Book A

CONNECTIONS

A Complete Course for Key Stage 3 Religious Studies

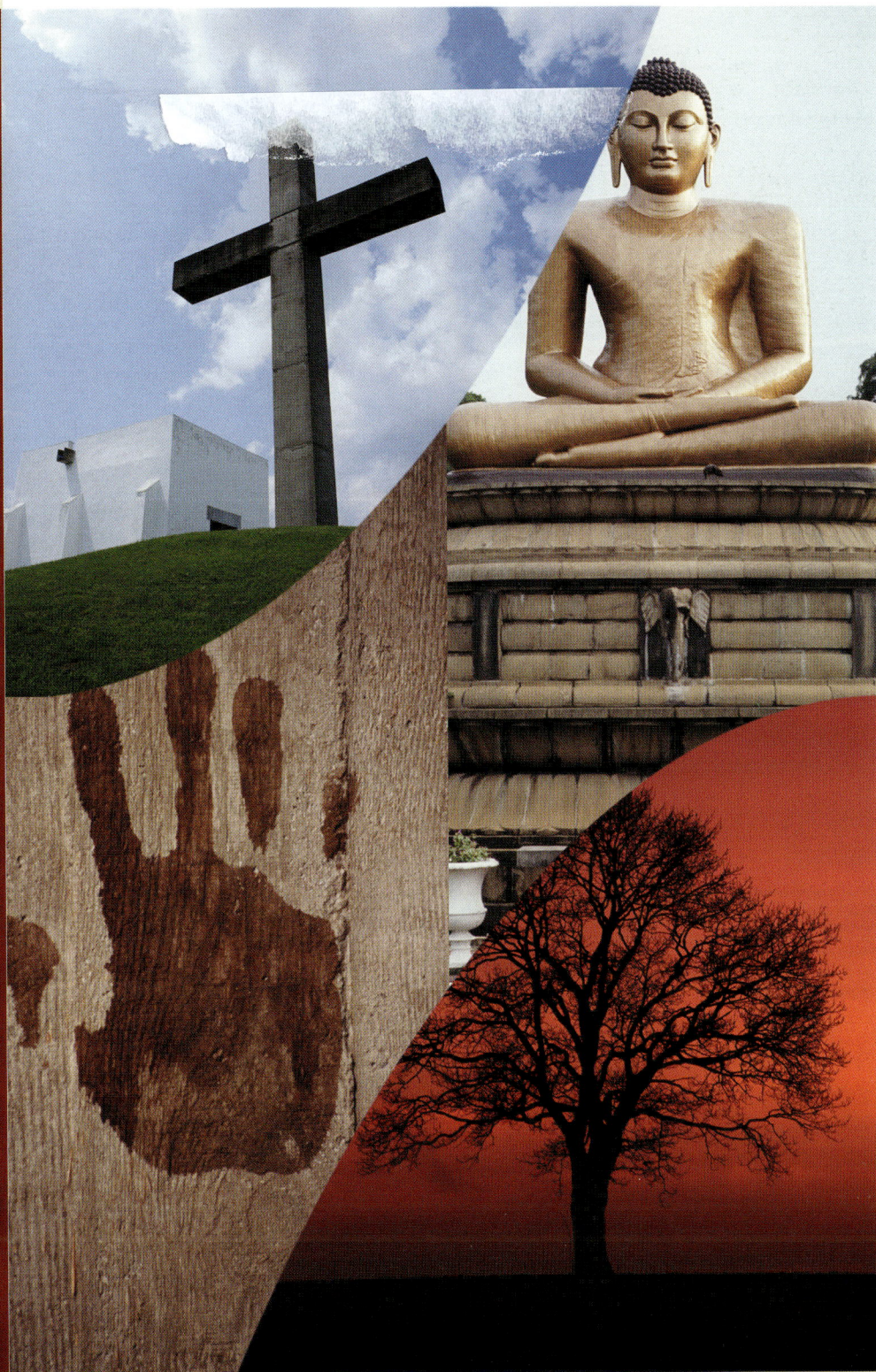

Libby Ahluwalia, Ann Lovelace, Jon Mayled, Joe Walker, Joy White

Hodder & Stoughton

A MEMBER OF THE HODDER HEADLINE GROUP

Acknowledgements

The publishers would like to thank the following individuals, institutions and companies for permission to reproduce copyright images in this book:
Cover photos reproduced courtesy of Photodisc.
Associated Press/Dexter Cruez, p55 (top right); Nigel Cattlin/Holt Studios International, p4 (middle, centre row); Bruce Coleman, p4 (right, centre row); Bruce Coleman collection/Marie Read, p4 (left, bottom row); Bruce Coleman/Kim Taylor, p4 (middle, top row); Bruce Coleman/Pacific Stock, 4 (left, centre row); CIRCA Photo Library/John Smith; Corbis, p40; Corbis/Dave Houser, p4 (top right); Corbis/David and Peter Turnley, p20; Corbis/David Samuel Robbins; p54 (top left); Corbis/Gavin Rowell, p54 (bottom right); Corbis/Jack Fields, p55 (left); Corbis/Carmen Redondo, p44; Corbis/Flip Schulke, p23; Corbis/James L Amos, p61 (bottom); Corbis/Jeremy Homes, p42 (bottom left); Corbis/Luca I. Tetton, p42 (top left); Corbis/Michael S Lewis, p29 (bottom left); Corbis/Nik Wheeler, p6; Corbis/Sergio Dorantes, p29 (top left); Corbis/William Dow, p7; Corbis/Wolfgang Kaehler, p29 (top & bottom right), 58; Corbis/Earl & Nazima Kowall, p30; Corbis/Howard Davies, p2 (centre); Corbis/Kevin R Morris, p43 (top right); Corbis/Lindsay Hebberd, p54 (bottom left); Corbis/Philip Gould, p21; Corbis/Tim Page, p55 (bottom right); Life file, p2 (top left, top right, middle, bottom centre & bottom left), 4 (top row left, top right centre row), 42 – 43 (centre), 43 (bottom right), 61 (top); Ruth Nossek, 60; Peter Sanders, p32; Hodder Religious, p22; Photodisc, p9, 60; Popperfoto, p36 © Adrees Latif/Reuters, 53 (top left) © Ian Waldie/Reuters; Science Photo Library, p5; Still Pictures, p14 (top & bottom), 24, 59, 62; Werner Forman, 54 (top right); www.worldreligions.co.uk, 53.

The publishers would also like to thank the following for permission to reproduce material in this book:
Extract from Desmond Tutu *Crying in the Wilderness: The Struggle for Justice in South Africa*, Continuum, published by permission of The Continuum International Publishing Group Ltd; Biblical quotations taken from the *Holy Bible, New International Version*, © 1973, 1978, 1984 by International Bible Society, used by permission of Hodder & Stoughton Ltd, all rights reserved; Extract from Jackie Pullinger *Chasing the Dragon*, Hodder & Stoughton, reproduced by permission of Hodder & Stoughton Limited. Extraxts from *The Meaning of the Holy Qur'an* translated by 'Abdullah Yusuf 'Ali, reproduced with permission from Amana Publications, 10710 Tucker Sreet, Bettsville, Maryland USA.

Every effort has been made to trace and acknowledge ownership of copyright. The publishers will be glad to make suitable arrangements with any copyright holders whom it has not been able to contact.

Orders: please contact Bookpoint Ltd, 130 Milton Park, Abingdon, Oxon OX14 4SB. Telephone: (44) 01235 827720. Fax: (44) 01235 400454. Lines are open from 9.00 - 6.00, Monday to Saturday, with a 24 hour message answering service.

British Library Cataloguing in Publication Data
A catalogue record for this title is available from the British Library

ISBN 0 340 80484 X

First Published 2002
Impression number   10 9 8 7 6 5 4 3 2 1
Year   2007   2006   2005   2004   2003   2002

Printed in Italy for Hodder & Stoughton Educational, a division of Hodder Headline Plc, 338 Euston Road, London NW1 3BH.

CONTENTS

Why do so many people around the world believe in God? They admit that God cannot be seen, or heard, or touched. But they are so sure that there is a God that they are prepared to let this affect all aspects of their lives. It might affect ...

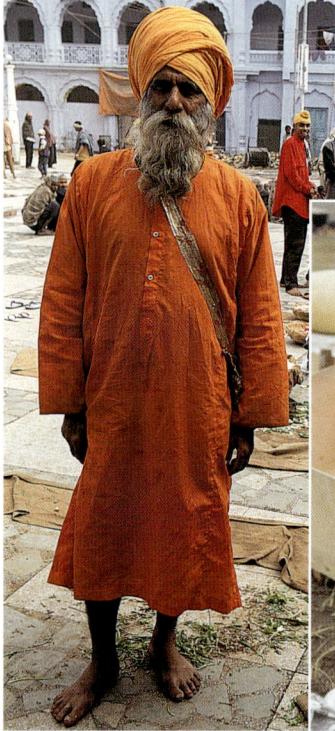

...the things they eat

...the way they dress

...the careers they choose

...what they do at weekends

...how they spend their money

...the way they bring up their children

...whom they marry

People who believe in God are called **theists**. But why do they think they are right, and that there really is a God? What makes them so convinced about God that they let their beliefs affect everything they do?

R. B. HALAL FOOD CENTRE
FRESH HALAL MEAT & POULTRY
34   Tel: 0181 – 672 5636   34

OXFAM

Language for learning

agnostic – an agnostic is someone who does not know whether there is a God or not

atheist – an atheist is someone who doesn't believe in God

theist – a theist is someone who believes in one God or many gods

STOP & Think

➤ Make a list of ways in which theists behave and think differently from people who are not religious at all. You might use the pictures to help you think of some ideas.

text message.........

We hold our beliefs for all different reasons. We believe some things because we have evidence for them. We believe other things because people tell us that they are true. Some things we believe because we have used our reason and worked out an answer, and other things are a matter of opinion.

People don't agree about where religious belief fits in. Some say there is evidence for the existence of God, some say we can work it out. Some people say that believing in God is a matter of personal opinion.

INTO action

❶ Look at the following statements. Some are true, and some are false:

  a The Eiffel Tower is in Paris.

  b Blue is the best colour for a school uniform.

  c It is raining today.

  d It is wrong to eat meat.

  e $2 \times 7 = 14$

  f Skiing holidays are more fun than beach holidays.

  g J. K. Rowling is a better writer than Shakespeare.

  h Tomorrow will be Wednesday.

Which ones do you think are true, and which ones are false? Compare your answers with the person sitting next to you.

❷ Looking back at your answers to question 1 – *how did you know* whether the statements were true or false? Is it because someone else told you, or because you used some of your five senses? Did you work it out, or is it your own opinion? Are you just going along with what everyone else thinks? Could anything make you change your mind about these statements?

The Big Picture

Does God exist? Why do people believe there is a God; what is their evidence, or how have they worked it out? In this unit, we will be looking at some of the arguments for and against the existence of God, and seeing why some people are convinced that there is a God while others are just as convinced that there isn't.

3

Many theists believe that the world around us demonstrates the existence of God. We do not have to guess whether or not God might exist, because there is evidence.

In nature, we can see many examples of beautiful shapes, colours and patterns. These do not look as if they just happen to have fallen into place; they look as though someone deliberately designed them that way, making them beautiful on purpose.

Nature is not only beautiful; it can also seem to be very clever. In nature we can see examples of things which appear to be perfectly designed to do whatever they need to do; for example:

- the pelican's beak is just right for carrying fish...

- the cactus and the camel are made so that they can keep reserve supplies of water in hot, dry climates...

- polar bears have thick warm white fur to keep out the cold and to camouflage them against the snow...

Even the planets move around in their orbits in mathematical patterns, as though a very clever engineer designed their movements.

Theists often argue that is impossible to believe that all this happened just by chance. They say that there is evidence in the world around us that the universe has been designed, by a great intelligence, which is God. This is often called

✋ STOP & Think ❓

the **Design Argument**, because people say that looking at the world around us gives us evidence that there is a God who designed it all.

The writers of the Bible sometimes wrote about the beauty and design of the world, and showed their belief that this was evidence for the existence of God. For example, in Psalm 19, the writer explains how the skies give evidence that God exists. He says that everyone all over the world can see the sky and see how it reveals that God exists, almost as though the sky has a voice and can speak about God for itself:

> *The heavens declare the glory of God;*
> *the skies proclaim the work of his hands.*
> *Day after day they pour forth speech;*
> *night after night they display knowledge.*

> *(Psalm 19:1–2)*

text message.........

Sometimes people use the example of the human eye to support their view that there must be a God. They talk about how the lens works just like the lens of a camera, and the retina at the back of the eye works just like film, sending images to the brain so that we can see. The pupil makes itself wider and narrower, according to the strength of the light, so that the images going to the brain are as sharp as possible.

Surely, they say, our eyes cannot have simply happened to exist, on their own, by chance. There must be a God, who designed the beauty of the world and everything in it.

⏸ PAUSE & RECORD 💿

- Make a collection of pictures from magazines or the Internet which show the beauty of nature, and the ways that animals and plants seem to have been designed. Make them into a collage poster, with the title 'Is there a God who designed all this?'.

When events are called natural disasters, it means that a tragedy has happened because of nature, such as an earthquake, a typhoon, a flood, a drought or a storm. It would not be a *natural* disaster if people were obviously to blame for it, for example an oil spillage from a tanker is not a *natural* disaster; and it would not be a natural *disaster* if no one was hurt and no damage was done, for example if a storm happened in the middle of the desert.

So a natural disaster is something caused by nature, which produces damage and suffering.

A natural disaster, such as an earthquake, is caused because of the structure of the world. Some people say that if God designed the world, he didn't design it very well.

Some people think that because natural disasters happen, this means that the world is not designed very well after all. Perhaps it means that the God who designed it is not very clever, or not very kind. What sort of a God would make a world where earthquakes and volcanoes kill innocent people? Or perhaps natural disasters mean that there is no God at all, and that good things and bad things just happen by accident.

What about things that are badly designed?

Sometimes, people point out that not everything in nature suggests an intelligent and loving God. Nature can be very cruel; for example, there are many animals which only survive by killing and eating other animals. They have sharp claws, teeth or beaks for ripping into the flesh of other creatures. They know how to look for the weakest prey, choosing sick or baby animals to kill because they will be the easiest to catch. They seem to have been designed to be cruel.

There is also fossil evidence of animals and plants which have died out (become extinct) because they were not designed in a way which helped them to survive. They could not cope with changes in climate or in habitat, and so they do not exist any more. Does this mean that God sometimes made designs which were mistakes, and did not work very well?

And what about other aspects of nature, such as disability, disease, and old age? Do these really suggest that there is a God who made it all happen, and planned it all this way? What about people who do really evil things – did God design the world so that some people are good and others are bad? What sort of a God would deliberately make a world with evil, suffering, ugliness and decay as part of the design?

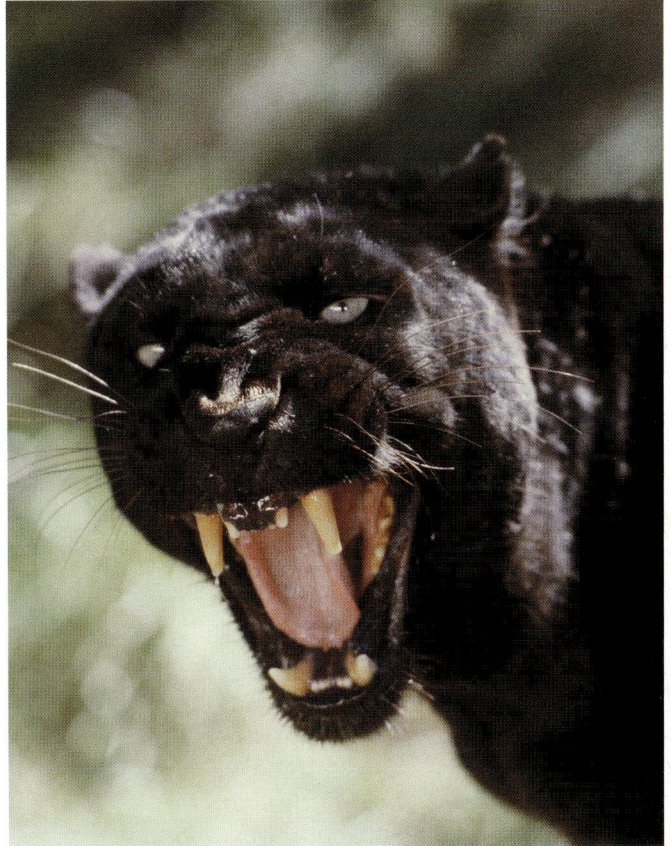

text message.........

The Design Argument has weaknesses, because not everything in the world is beautiful, and not everything seems to work perfectly. If we try to look at nature to see evidence for God, it can suggest that God does not care whether people or animals suffer. Or it can suggest that God makes mistakes and designs things badly, or that God has no control when things go wrong.

The Cosmological Argument

Sometimes people say that they know God exists, just because the universe exists and everything around us is moving and changing all the time. Theists sometimes say that nothing would exist unless something or somebody had made it. The universe exists; so there must be a creator who made the universe, and this creator must be God. This is known as the **Cosmological Argument** – the cosmos is another name for the universe.

Most of the world's religions say that the universe exists because God made it:

And among his signs is the creation of the heavens and the Earth.

(Surah 30:22, from the Qur'an, the holy book of the Muslim religion)

The earth is the Lord's, and everything in it, the world, and all who live in it
For he founded it upon the seas
and established it upon the waters.

(Psalm 24:1–2, from the Bible, the holy book of Jews and Christians)

God is the beginning and end of everything. He is the Designer and Creator.

(Guru Gobind Singh, a holy teacher from the Sikh religion)

Most theists believe that there must have been something which started off the whole universe. There must have been a beginning – a starting point – and this starting point had to be something which is eternal – it has no beginning and no end. It had to be something with enormous power, and the ability to do absolutely everything. Theists say that God is omnipotent, which means all-powerful – there

is nothing that God cannot do. The Cosmological Argument says that things only move when they have been moved by some-

Language for learning

cosmology – the study of the universe

omnipotent – all-powerful, able to do anything at all

STOP & Think

➤ Imagine a domino standing on its end on a table. The next moment, it is lying down flat. What do you think must have happened to make the domino fall over? Could it have fallen over if nothing had happened at all?

thing else. If nothing moves them, then they just stay still and do nothing. We can see that the universe is moving; the planets go around in orbits in their galaxies, and the universe is expanding. What started all this movement? We know that nothing starts moving unless something else is making it move – so, some people say, this shows there must be a God who put everything into action.

Does this argument work?

Some people disagree with the Cosmological Argument, because they say that perhaps the universe had no beginning – maybe it has just always existed. Perhaps things can just start moving, or just come into existence, by themselves. Some of the latest discoveries by scientists suggest that this can happen, and atoms can suddenly appear out of nowhere.

Sometimes atheists say that God is an old-fashioned idea. They argue that religious people say that God did something, when they just mean 'we don't know how it happened'. Atheists say that religious people use the idea of God to explain things that they don't understand, when they should be trying to find out rather than accepting that the world is a mystery. They say that the more we learn, the less we need the idea of God to explain things.

But theists argue that although scientists can often explain how things happen, this does not remove the need for God. Some scientists find that the more they learn about the universe, the stronger their belief becomes, because they realise how wonderfully everything fits together.

For many people, the fact that the universe exists is enough to convince them that there must be a God. Scientific explanations might be able to tell us how the universe began, but they think we must be here for a reason. Only belief in God can give an explanation of why we are here at all.

Other people think that there is no reason for our existence. The universe happened by accident. We are only here because of chance. There is no need to look for God to explain anything.

text message.........

Scientists usually believe that the universe was started when a Big Bang exploded, causing matter to fly out in all directions. As the matter cooled down, it formed the stars and the planets, which began to move in orbits because of the forces of gravity. Some scientists think that this explanation of how the universe began is enough, and there is no need to bring God into it. Others think that we still need to know what made the Big Bang happen in the first place.

RewindRewind**Rewind**

Look back at the Design Argument. Do you think it is stronger or weaker than the Cosmological Argument? Or do you think they are both strong, or both weak?

Theists say that it is possible to learn about God from looking around us, and that everyone can see this evidence. But they also believe that God makes himself known to some people in a special, more individual way. Some people say that they have direct, personal experience of meeting God. They know that God exists because they have met him. They have also heard stories of other people who have experienced God, and they think that these people can be trusted to be telling the truth.

Some people say that they have seen God in **visions**.

> There was a shining light, and I saw a figure stretching her hands towards me and telling me not to be frightened.

Sometimes people say that they have **heard God speaking** to them as a voice.

> I didn't know what I should do as a career, but one day I heard a voice telling me that I should become a nurse and go and work in a poor country. So that's what I did.

Some people have had **conversion experiences**, where they have become convinced that God exists, and this has changed their way of life.

> I suddenly felt as though a huge weight had been lifted from me, and I felt a great warmth which I knew was the love of God. From then on I became a different person, and now I go to church every Sunday.

Sometimes people believe that through **meditation** they have come to a deeper understanding of God.

> After I had been quiet for a long time, I began to realise that all the people, plants and animals are somehow connected together as parts of nature.

Sometimes people feel especially **close to God**, for example when they are in trouble, or when they are in a special holy place, or when they are alone.

> *Whenever I've got worries about money or about my children, I go to the mosque. I feel that I can talk to Allah when I'm there, and I know Allah listens to me.*

Sometimes people believe that they have experienced God through being **healed**, or through receiving **answers to prayer**.

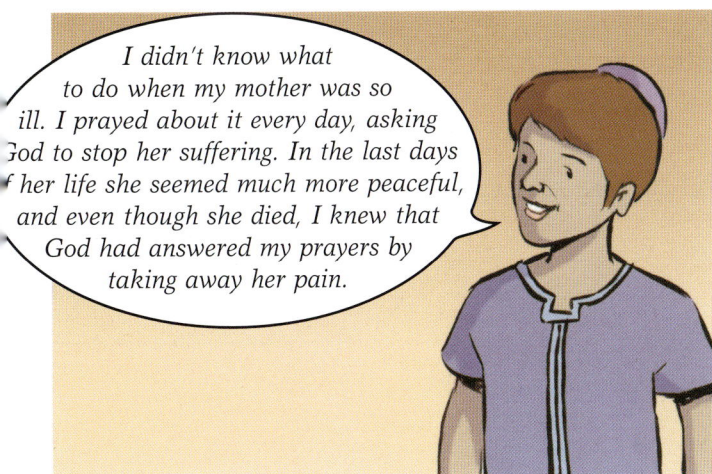

> *I didn't know what to do when my mother was so ill. I prayed about it every day, asking God to stop her suffering. In the last days of her life she seemed much more peaceful, and even though she died, I knew that God had answered my prayers by taking away her pain.*

A lot of these religious experiences are very personal. Only the person who had the experience felt it happen, and often, it was so different from other kinds of experiences that it is difficult to put into words and share with other people. But often, the experience is so strongly felt that it makes the theist convinced of the existence of God.

Language for learning

conversion – when someone completely changes his or her thinking and way of life, often because of a religious experience

Does religious experience prove anything?

If someone has an experience that they think has come from God, it can be very powerful and convincing for them. But other people might be less sure. They might think that it was all a dream, or some kind of hallucination. They might think that religious people want God to exist, and so they think they have experienced God, but really it is all in their imaginations. Religious experiences are too private to prove anything, because no one can test them to see if they really happened, or if they really came from God. But even if they can't prove anything, they can still be useful, because if lots of people have a similar experience it might suggest that there is more to it than imagination or wishful thinking.

STOP & Think

➤ What would you think if your best friend told you that he or she had experienced God in some way?

Where do we look for God?

End of Unit Activities

What do you know?

1. What do the following words mean: **atheist** **theist** **agnostic** ?
2. In your own words, explain what the Design Argument says.
3. Why do some people disagree with the Design Argument?
4. What reason does the Cosmological Argument give for the existence of God?
5. Why do some people disagree with the Cosmological Argument?
6. What do people mean when they say that they have had a religious experience?
7. How might a religious person's lifestyle be different from the lifestyle of someone who wasn't religious?
8. Is it possible to prove that there is a God, or to prove that there isn't?

What do you think?

Copy the chart below, filling in the blank boxes to show whether you agree or disagree with these reasons for belief in God. Try to give a reason for your views.

Reasons people give for belief in God:	My opinion:
Everything in the world seems to be so well suited to its purpose that there must be someone who designed it that way.	
Some people say that they have seen or heard God directly, and they would not say this unless it were true.	
We all have a sense of right and wrong, so there must be a God who gives us our consciences.	
There must be a God who rewards us in heaven if we behave well, or punishes us if we behave badly, otherwise leading a good life would be pointless.	
The universe exists, so there must be a God who started it off. It could not have just started by itself from nothing.	

action INTO

❶ Make a questionnaire to use with your friends, teachers or family. Ask questions which try to find out whether people believe in God, and their reasons why or why not. Try your questionnaire on four or five different people, and think of a way in which to present your results.

❷ Make a poster to illustrate different views about whether or not there is a God. Divide your page in half – on one side, write 'There must be a God, because…' and on the other side 'There can't be a God, because…'. Use writing and illustrations to show different reasons for or against belief in God.

❸ Design and act out a role play where different people exchange views about whether or not God exists. Think of some interesting characters – an astronomer? Someone who takes emergency aid to the victims of natural disasters? A priest? A scientist?

❹ Find out more about people who claim to have had religious experiences. You might research one of the following:

St Bernadette	**Guru Nanak**
Muhammad ﷺ	**John Wesley**
Julian of Norwich	**Isaiah**

Justice?

Fourteen year old Cameron left the house that day for school as normal... well, if you can call his life normal. His mum was lying in bed probably still drunk. Dad hadn't come home last night... again. Who knows where he might be. Cameron got his two younger brothers out of bed. Sleepily he made them some breakfast. He made sure they had the right clothes for school. He fixed them some sandwiches and a snack for later. He walked them to school. Halfway there he remembered he'd forgotten his reading book. Cameron made them wait while he ran back to get it. He then made sure the boys went in to school. It wouldn't be the first time they'd run off and missed a day's classes. Cameron would have to write a note for them. They'd get it from Dad if he found out.

By the time Cameron got to school he was pretty tired. History first thing. He had no pencil, he'd just plain forgotten to pack one in his bag this morning. Mr Thomas, the history teacher spoke "Where's your pencil Cameron?" Cameron could only mumble an apology.

Mr Thomas went on, much more loudly... "NO PENCIL!? WHAT'S THE USE OF COMING TO SCHOOL WITHOUT ONE? DO YOU THINK I HAVE NOTHING BETTER TO DO THAN TO RUN AROUND HANDING OUT PENCILS TO PEOPLE WHO CAN'T BE BOTHERED TO BRING THEIR OWN?..."
Cameron lowered his head.

It's not fair!

How many times have you said this? What was the problem? Why did you feel it wasn't fair? Justice is when we are treated for who we are, no matter what we look like, sound like, or where we live or what we do. Justice is when we are treated 'right'.

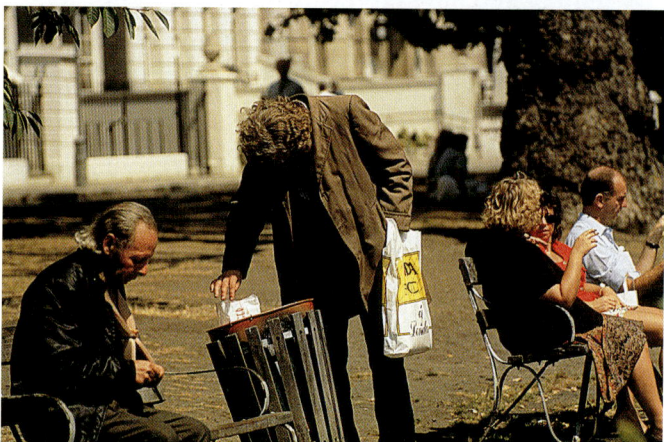

STOP & Think ?

➤ **Was Mr Thomas being fair? How could he have shown more justice to Cameron?**

PAUSE & RECORD

- **Imagine you are the Head Teacher in Cameron's school. One of the pupils has reported what Mr Thomas said to Cameron. You know about Cameron's hard life. What would you say to Mr Thomas?**

Jesus on justice

Zacchaeus lived at the time of Jesus. He was a tax-collector. He collected money from his own people, the Jews, to give to the enemy, the hated Romans. He heard that Jesus was coming to visit his home town. He decided to go and see what all the fuss was about this man from Nazareth.

As he moved along with the crowd, he was jostled and pushed. It was a busy crowd, and he was only a small man. But he was sure quite a few of them would have been getting a little dig of their elbows in more than they needed to. No one liked him much.

What was he thinking?...

I'd heard all about this Jesus. They said he was God's son. They said he did amazing things. Yeah, yeah. I've seen it all before. Another con-man trying to make some money. Everyone's the same, eh? I thought I might learn a trick or two from him. Hey, stop pushing me... these ignorant peasants. They just don't get it. We can't beat the Romans – so at least we should make some money out of them. So what if I take money from my own people and give it to the Romans? If I don't, someone else will. Maybe I take a little bit for myself too, but why shouldn't I? It's a dangerous job. I deserve it. All this and I can only see the top of Jesus' head... move out of my way, don't you know who I am? Oh for goodness sake. I'll nip up this little tree here, then I'll get a better look. That's it, clearer now. Where I should be... above them all. Yes you can look at me peasants. I may be small, but I'm not the one with no money am I?

Here's Jesus now. He's stopping. Turning around. Looking at me. Here we go. He's going to get the crowd going. Look at the small man, he'll say. An enemy of the Jews. If you want to know how not to live your life, look at him. The enemy of God's people who wants to see the show! Get ready for the laughs, the jeers, the spitting. But his face shows no anger. He just looks. I feel a little embarrassed. Everyone is looking at me, but just waiting. Come down Zacchaeus! But how does he know me? I shall eat dinner at your house tonight, my friend... Friend? They all look as confused as I feel. But he means it. I feel a little ashamed. This man knows me.

Jesus did go to Zacchaeus' house and have dinner. Zacchaeus found the whole experience changed him completely.

✋ STOP & Think ❓

➤ Was Jesus' treatment of Zacchaeus just?

➤ What might the people Zacchaeus had robbed think of Jesus making friends with him?

➤ What do you think Jesus should have done?

➤ Why do you think Zacchaeus reacted to Jesus so strongly?

Dear Paul...

Who was Paul?

The very first Christians didn't have it easy. They were sometimes picked on. Sometimes they were treated very badly. Even killed. Paul didn't like them. He did everything he could to make their lives a misery. One day, on the road to a city called Damascus, he had a vision of Jesus. After this, he stopped attacking the Christians. In fact, he became one! He wrote many letters to the new Christians all over the world. In these he tried to give them advice about how to live as Christians. Because of this he became one of the best-known Christians. His letters are now part of the Bible. This problem page looks at some modern problems – but with a difference.

What would Paul say?

Dear Paul,
Someone has been calling me names at school. My big brother says he'll get him for me, and my brother is BIG. Should I let him sort this out for me?

Ben (12)

Dear Ben,
I was once thrown into prison for nothing. They beat me up pretty badly. But God helped me. The man who put me in jail was a bit scared. I think he thought I was going to get God to strike him down or something! He nearly killed himself he was so scared. But what would be the point in getting him back? So I talked with him, and he became a Christian too. Talk with this person. Show him you're not so bad really. Let him know you could've caused him harm but chose not to.
You never know…

(See Acts 16:16–40.)

Dear Paul,
The boys in my class won't let me play football with them. They know I can play as well as them (maybe better!), but they just don't want a girl in the team. What should I do?

Alice (11)

Dear Alice,
Even in my time, some men weren't very nice to women. They thought men were better than women. Of course, we didn't have football then (at least, not like yours!). I told them that they should treat each other as equals. Jesus cares for us all, whether we're boys or girls. The boys should be like Jesus. They should see you for who you are – a good footballer. Why does it matter to them that you're a girl? You're just as much a human being as them!

(See Galatians 3:28.)

Dear Paul,

My friend helps out at a charity shop every weekend. It's to help the homeless. He wants me to help. We're both Christians, but I'm not sure about helping. You see, I have to admit it. I think most of these people begging on the streets are just wasters. They just annoy me. They should get a job or something. I know I'm supposed to love everyone as a Christian but it's not easy. They'd deserve my love better if they did something for themselves sometimes. What should I do?

Gavin (13)

Dear Gavin,

Mmmm, you do have a problem don't you? Yes you're right, Christians should love everyone no matter who they are. But there's more. I think love is patient and kind, it's not selfish, it's not full of itself, it doesn't judge people for what's happened in the past. It doesn't just let bad things happen, it does something about them. I think you need to forget about why these people are on the streets. It can be complicated. Just show them love, and see what happens…

(See 1 Corinthians 13.)

Dear Paul,

There's a boy in my class who's really got it in for me. I can't do anything right. He's always making fun of me in front of others. But I've got him now. I've found out that he's really bad at sports, and I'm really good. So I'll challenge him to a race… then I'll really show him up for the idiot he is. What do you think?

Gerry (12)

Dear Gerry,

No, I don't think that's a very good idea at all. In fact, I think it'll just make people feel bad about you! Revenge gets you nowhere. If this boy is your enemy, treat him with kindness. Share your sweets with him. Don't make a fool of him. It'll just make you look bad. Be nice to him. This should make him feel ashamed that he's been so horrible to you. He might even change his ways.

(See Romans 12:17–21.)

Paul on justice

- Forgive people for the wrong they do
- Don't take revenge
- Treat everyone as equals
- Be fair to everyone
- Don't judge people
- Show love and concern for everyone

17

How can we tell?

Jesus taught a lot about justice. Sometimes his teaching was in **stories**, like the parables. Sometimes his teaching about justice was shown by what he **did**. Sometimes he just came right out and **said** what he thought. Paul used these teachings to work out what justice was. So do modern Christians. Here's a 'questionnaire' which asks you to work out what Jesus would do. Go to the bible text for answers. You should do this in groups and discuss your choices.

1. Someone is picking on you because of how you look. You really don't like him. You get the chance to get him back. Do you...

   a. *take the chance and really enjoy it?*
   b. *ignore it and carry on hating the person?*
   c. *try to like the person and make friends with him?*
   d. *do something else?*

See Luke 6:27–35.

2. A soldier in battle finds one of the enemy lying injured – close to death. It's the same man who yesterday killed three of the soldier's friends. What should he do?

   a. *take him to the field hospital so that the doctors can save him*
   b. *ignore him – let him die slowly*
   c. *finish the man off – he doesn't deserve to live*
   d. *something else*

See Luke 10:25–37.

3. A man's teenage son gets in with a bad crowd. He's always getting into trouble. They take the man's car for a joy-ride and wreck it. The son realises that he's gone too far. What should his dad do?

   a. *have the son charged by the police. It'll teach him a lesson*
   b. *accept his son's mistake and start over again*
   c. *throw the son out of the house and never speak to him again*
   d. *something else*

See Luke 15:11–31.

4. A woman wins the lottery. What should she do?

   a. *keep all the money for herself*
   b. *give it all away to the poor*
   c. *keep most of it and give a little away*
   d. *something else*

See Luke 18:18–29.

5. You are a doctor in question 2. The enemy soldier has been brought to you. But you're not sure if you should bother trying to save him – he's your enemy after all, and not one of your people. What would you do?

   a. *just leave him, you've enough to do*
   b. *do your best to help him, he's human after all*
   c. *give him drugs to finish him off*
   d. *something else*

See Luke 7:1–10.

Justice for Jesus

Christians don't always think that the teaching of Jesus is easy. It can be especially hard to follow when it's about justice. Jesus' teaching on justice seems to be…

- Don't take revenge
- Forgive people for what they've done wrong
- Use your wealth to help others whenever possible
- Treat everyone as equals
- Be fair to everyone
- Don't judge people
- Show love and concern for everyone

*Rewind**Rewind**Rewind*

How do these compare with Paul's teachings about justice on page 17?

You do to me…

Some people think that everything Jesus teaches about justice is summed up in the following passage:

[Jesus said to his disciples]

I was hungry and you fed me.

I was thirsty and you gave me a drink.

I was a stranger and you took me into your homes.

I was naked and you put clothes on me.

I was sick and you took care of me.

I was in prison and you visited me.

The disciples replied;

When Lord did we ever see you hungry and feed you or thirsty and give you a drink?

When did we ever see you a stranger and bring you into our homes?

When did we ever see you naked and give you our clothes?

When did we ever see you sick and care for you?

When did we see you in prison and visit you?

[Jesus said]

Whenever you did this for the least important person, you did it for me.

Matthew 25:35–46.

STOP & Think

➤ **What does Jesus mean here?**

19

Desmond Tutu

Desmond Tutu was an Anglican Archbishop in South Africa. All his life he has fought against injustice. In South Africa there used to be apartheid. This was where the Government treated people differently depending on what colour they were. In South Africa, this meant that the whites ran the country, even though there weren't that many whites there. Black people were badly treated. They couldn't vote, didn't get paid as much as whites, and were much poorer. They could only live in certain areas. These were always much poorer than the white areas. Desmond thought this was wrong. He believed that no one should have a hard life just because of their skin colour. In 1988, the Government at the time got much stricter. He ended up in prison. Eventually South Africa changed and whites and blacks became equals.

Desmond was put in charge of something called the 'Truth and Reconciliation Committee', by the new President, Nelson Mandela. This committee was to bring people together who had done wrong and people who'd been badly treated during the apartheid years. During apartheid, blacks and whites had done many terrible things to each other. There had been a lot of injustice. Desmond said that revenge was no use. People had to forgive and move on. Desmond's Christian faith helped him do what he thought was right. South Africa learned to live with its past.

Desmond still lives in South Africa. He's retired but still working hard wherever he finds injustice.

I long and work for a South Africa which is open and just; where people count, and where they will have equal access to the good things in life.

Desmond Tutu, 'Crying in the Wilderness.'

What does Desmond believe about justice?

Everyone is equal in the sight of God

- So everyone should have the same chances in life

- No one should suffer because of where they live or what their skin colour is

- Compassion, care and love for each other are some of the highest things people can feel for each other

- It is the responsibility of the strong to look after the weak

- You should use your wealth wisely. No one should be so poor that it threatens their life. Everyone should be fairly rewarded for their efforts

- Forgiving is much better than taking revenge

RewindRewind**Rewind**

Which of the teachings about justice (Jesus' or Paul's) might Desmond use to explain why he did what he did?

Mother Teresa of Calcutta

Mother Theresa was a Yugoslavian nun who ended up working in the slums of Calcutta in India. She believed that everyone was a child of God. She said that she saw Jesus in everyone she helped. Her order, the Sisters of Charity, help people in Calcutta who are homeless, very poor, usually very ill, and sometimes dying. Most of these people live on the streets. They have no one to care for them and no money to help them get treatment for their illnesses. Mother Teresa became world famous. She travelled the world getting money for her work with the poor. She met with Kings and Queens, Presidents, and World leaders. But she always returned as soon as she could to Calcutta. Here, she herself would tend to the sick and the dying. A small woman who had the courage to do things for people which would make some of us ill even to think about. She set up other homes and hospitals all over the world. In 1996 she died. The Roman Catholic Church is deciding whether or not to make her a Saint.

What did Mother Teresa believe about justice?

- Everyone deserves love and kindness
- Everyone matters to God and so should matter to everyone else
- People should be helped no matter what has caused their problems
- No one is above helping others
- Everyone deserves the same chances in life, whether they are rich or poor
- It is a duty for the strong to help the weak

RewindRewind**Rewind**

Which of the teachings about justice (Jesus' or Paul's) might Mother Teresa have used to explain why she did what she did?

When I look after the sick,
I am looking after Jesus.

Mother Teresa

Jackie Pullinger

As a young girl, Jackie Pullinger went to Hong Kong. She ended up living and working in a place called the Walled City. It was a rough place, filled with crime, violence and gang wars. Many terrible things happened here. Jackie said, 'One name for the Walled City is Hak Nam. In English, "Darkness". As I began to know it better I learned how true this was... it was a place of terrible darkness both physical and spiritual... when you meet the men and women who have to live and suffer in such a place, you can be broken by compassion' (*Chasing the Dragon* p34). Jackie decided to stay and help the people who lived there. She set up a small church and a club inside the Walled City. Gradually people came to this club because they learned that Jackie cared about them as people. Many were drug addicts or members of very violent gangs known as the Triads. Many stopped committing crimes and being violent. Some also gave up drugs. They became Christians and helped Jackie with her work.

Jackie believes that everyone matters to God. No matter what they have done they can be forgiven by God and start a new life.

Jesus loves you. He doesn't love the things you've done, but he loves you.

Jackie speaking to one of the Triad gang members

What does Jackie believe about justice?

- Everyone deserves a chance in life

- People can be forgiven no matter what they've done, if they ask and agree not to do wrong again

- You should show God's love to everyone, no matter who they are or what their life is like

- People who are poor and have a hard life should be helped so that they can live a full life.

RewindRewind**Rewind**

Which of the teachings about justice (Jesus' or Paul's) might Jackie Pullinger have used to explain why she did what she did?

PAUSE & RECORD

- Design a short information leaflet about one of these three Christians. Follow this format:

Side 1

A BIBLE STORY THIS PERSON MIGHT FOLLOW IN HIS/HER WORK	DRAWING OF THE PERSON OR SOMETHING ABOUT THEIR LIFE

INFORMATION ABOUT THE PERSON	INFORMATION ABOUT WHAT HE/SHE DOES/DID

Side 2

Martin Luther King

Martin fought for equal rights for black people in some of the States of the USA. This was in the 1960s. Here there was apartheid too. Black people couldn't sit in certain cafes, shop in certain shops, or even walk in some parks. 'Whites only' signs were very common. This was called racial segregation. Martin organised people to oppose this. They wanted to end it. They staged 'sit-ins', 'freedom rides', protest marches. Martin was beaten and put in prison many times. Some people were killed. But Martin never asked the black people to take revenge. He taught non-violent resistance.

Everything he managed to do he did peacefully. There were great changes. Many of the States accepted desegregation. Blacks were allowed in to places they hadn't been before. They didn't have to give up their seats for white people on the buses any more. But Martin paid a heavy price for his belief in justice and equality. On 4 April 1968, he was shot and killed. All through his fight for justice he knew he could be killed. He did say that he wanted a long life, just like anyone else. But more than anything he wanted justice.

RewindRewind**Rewind**

Which of the teachings about justice (Jesus' or Paul's) might Martin Luther King have used to explain why he did what he did?

What did Martin believe about justice?

- All are equal in the sight of God
- It is our duty to bring justice where there's injustice
- People should be paid fairly for their work
- You should act with love and care towards everyone
- You should not fight against your enemies. You should show them the wrong they do and teach them how to change
- You should not suffer because of where you live or the colour of your skin

▌▌ PAUSE & RECORD

- Split a display board in your class into four sections. At the top, write 'What I think of...' Put the names of the four people you've studied in this section. Each person in the class should be anonymously allowed to write what they think and your teacher can put these on the board under the right name.

Christians believe that justice is very important. They also believe that the world is still full of injustice. What examples of injustice are there in the world today?

Poverty

- World wide, 800 million people go to bed hungry every day

- 1.75 billion people don't have safe water to drink

- The world bank says that about 1.3 billion people earn less than $1 a day

I haven't had a day's rest for two months, and I work from 8am to 9 or 10 at night, sometimes even the whole night through. That's why I'm ill, my head feels heavy... The bosses don't pay us properly. They'll say you've only done 30 or 40 hours in a month, when you've really done 150. There's no record, so they can say what they like.

Bangladeshi worker quoted on CAFOD Website

Inequality

- The United Nations says women are 50% of the world's population. They are 30% of the working population, they do 65% of the working hours and get only 10% of the world's income.

- Many blacks in the USA believe that equal rights is not yet complete. They point to the small number of blacks in well-paid professional jobs compared to whites.

- Many people say that you're treated differently in Britain if you haven't gone to the 'right' school.

Martin Luther King's dream hasn't come true yet. You only have to look at America's prisons. There are far more black people in them than white. Does this mean we're not so good as the whites? Of course not. You're more likely to turn to crime if your life is hard. And your life is more likely to be hard if you're black. Just like it's always been.

African American

Homelessness

- There are around 100 million homeless people in the world today.

- 40% of Britain's homeless were thrown out of their houses by parents or relatives.

- Around 32 million of the world's homeless are street-children.

I was born on the streets. I'll probably die on the streets. It's all I know now. I don't worry for me, but I worry for my little brother. He's 7. He's not really my brother, I just found him, so I suppose he is my family now. I look after him. But I have to leave him on his own sometimes while I make some money. I beg, I steal. I make money in other ways too. Not much. But we eat something every day. Lots of the other street-kids don't.

Maria, Brazilian street-kid, 13 years old

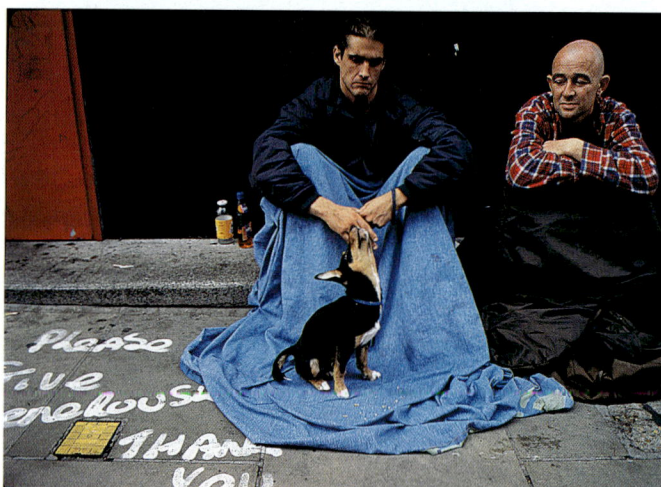

What do Christians do?

Christians want to live in a world where there's justice. Sometimes you have to work hard to make this happen. Christians believe that they should try to bring God's Kingdom here on earth. This means making the world the way God wants it. The largest single provider of health care and social services in the world is the Christian Church. Christian organisations work hard to bring justice. They make their money entirely from what is given to them by the general public.

Christian Aid – 'We believe in Life before death'

Christian Aid was started by churches in Britain and Ireland in 1945. After the war, many people were poor and homeless. Christian Aid was set up to help them. Most of its work is now in the developing world. It tries to do three things:

❶ Help people to help themselves by giving them what they need to be independent.

❷ Challenge the causes of poverty and injustice.

❸ Show governments and ordinary people that we can all make a difference to the lives of the poor and oppressed.

Christian Aid raises money here and gives it to local communities in poor countries. Local people decide the best way to use it. Christian Aid thinks this is best. Its *partners* in poorer countries make their own decisions, because they know best how the money should be used to make life better.

In the year 2000, it raised 57,692,000 pounds.

Christian Aid also campaigns for the poor. For example its campaign, 'Trade for Life' tries to show how international trade is good for the rich but not so good for the poor. It shows how world trade always seems to work in favour of the rich. Christian Aid believes that you can't just tackle the effects of poverty and injustice, you've got to tackle the causes too. Christian Aid helps anyone who needs help – not just Christians. On the Christian Aid Website, Jo, a Christian Aid volunteer explains why she helps:

> I am a Christian and I believe that Jesus always cared for poor people. The Bible is full of stories which show us this. Jesus gave Christians two great commandments: to love God and our neighbours. I see our neighbours as all our brothers and sisters around the world. That is why I support Christian Aid.

PAUSE & RECORD

Christian ♦ Aid
We believe in life before death

- Find out about the work of Christian aid world-wide (visit www.christian-aid.org.uk).
  In what ways does it work to bring justice?

What do you know?

❶ Write one example you have found in this unit which shows *injustice*.

❷ In your own words, explain what happens in the Zacchaeus story, and what the message in the story is.

❸ In your own words, describe what Paul thinks about equality.

❹ From one of the gospel sections listed on pages 16–18, write two things Jesus taught about justice.

❺ Who was Desmond Tutu, and how did he work for justice?

❻ Think of the four modern people you've studied in this unit. Write two beliefs about justice they'd all agree on.

❼ From your study of this unit, what do you think is the greatest *injustice* in the world today?

What do you think?

❶ On a display board in your class, draw a large tree. Each person in your class should use a piece of paper of one colour to write down one **cause** of injustice in the world today. These should then be stuck on the roots of the tree. Another colour should be used to show the **effects** of injustice. These should be stuck on the trunk of the tree. You should then use another colour of paper to write one **response** to injustice. These should be stuck on as leaves. Your example of injustice could be personal, in your area or worldwide. Responses to injustice could be personal or by some of the people/organisations you have studied in this section.

❷ You should also write one example of what you could do to help the world achieve justice. This should be displayed in your classroom under the heading, 'What can I do?'

❸ Find out more about one of the people/organisations who have responded to justice. Using coloured paper, or tracing paper which you colour, design a 'stained-glass' window based on this person/organisation. Perhaps your teacher will display these in your classroom on the window.

❹ In groups, draw up a list of things which would make the world a fairer place. You should write these out to look like a legal document. Use the title, 'Seven steps to a fairer world'.

❺ Choose one of the examples of injustice you have studied. In groups, compose a song or a poem about it. This should show what the problem is as well as suggest how it could be fixed.

action INTO

❶ Imagine one of the people you've studied in this unit came to your school assembly. What would they say about justice and injustice in the world today? Write a short speech they might give. You might also like to get your teacher to arrange for you to show some slides with this speech.

❷ Write to, or invite in to speak to your class, your local Christian Minister/Vicar/Priest/Pastor. Prepare a list of questions you would ask him/her to find out what Christians in your area are doing to bring justice into the world.

❸ Find out how you (or your school) could help make the world a fairer, more just place. Perhaps you could organise an event.

❹ Make up your own questionnaire about justice. See if you can get your local Minister/Vicar/Priest/Pastor to get his/her congregation to complete it.

❺ Make up a TV news report on the story of Zacchaeus (page 15). How would you report it? Include interviews with people in the crowd as well as Zacchaeus himself. Why did this event change him so much?

Final thoughts

This unit has explored the idea of justice and what it means for Christians. Now think about how this applies to you. What difference can you make to the world?

Copy and complete the following:

Three things I could do to make the world a more just place...

❶ _____

❷ _____

❸ _____

Answer the following:

In this unit:

a. What have you enjoyed the best?

b. What did you not enjoy?

c. How good was your work?

d. What would you have liked to improve?

Now think of three questions about justice in the world that you would like to find the answers to.

Most religions have a founder. A founder is someone who starts something – your school may have a founder for example. Some places remember their founders every year by having a special celebration called Founder's Day.

In religions, a founder is a person who was responsible for teaching people about the religion right at the beginning and explaining to them how God wanted them to live their lives.

You may already know about founders of some other religions. Abraham is sometimes called the founder of Judaism because God chose him and told him that if he obeyed God's teachings he would become the founder of a great nation. Abraham followed God's instructions and took all his family, servants and cattle and moved to a different country where he and his family and their descendants could follow God's teachings.

Guru Nanak Dev Ji founded Sikhism. Nanak had been brought up as a Hindu in the Punjab (in India) where there were many Hindus and Muslims. Nanak was very religious and very intelligent. He believed that God wanted everyone to follow the same teachings and taught that there was 'no Hindu and no Muslim' – everyone was equal in front of God. He formed a new religion for his followers which was called Sikhism. A Sikh is a 'disciple' – someone who follows God's teachings.

In both cases these were very religious people who believed that they had received a message from God about how people should live their lives and follow God's teachings.

There are other founders such as Jesus and the Buddha. Although Jesus could be called the founder of Christianity, Christians believe that he was the Son of God and came to earth in order to teach people about God. Siddatha Gotama, the Buddha, was a very religious man who wanted to find an answer to why people suffered and spent many years thinking and meditating about this.

In this unit we are looking at the founder of Islam, the Prophet Muhammad ﷺ. The symbol ﷺ which follows the name of the Prophet throughout this unit is in Arabic, the language of Islam. It stands for the words 'Salla-illahu alaiha wa sallam' – 'peace and blessings of Allah upon him'. These words are said by Muslims each time they mention the Prophet's name as a sign of respect.

Obviously, Muhammad ﷺ, his life and teachings are very important to Muslims and this unit will be considering important times and events in his life as well as some of the teachings which he gave to his followers.

By learning about Muhammad ﷺ and his teachings we can also learn more about the religion of Islam.

✋ STOP & Think ❓

➤ What is a founder?

➤ What other founders can you think of?

➤ Why do you think it might be important to know about the founder of a religion?

➤ Explain why Muslims think that it is important to show respect to Muhammad ﷺ by using this symbol after his name.

The teachings of Muhammad ﷺ are very important to Muslims and are followed by people all over the world.

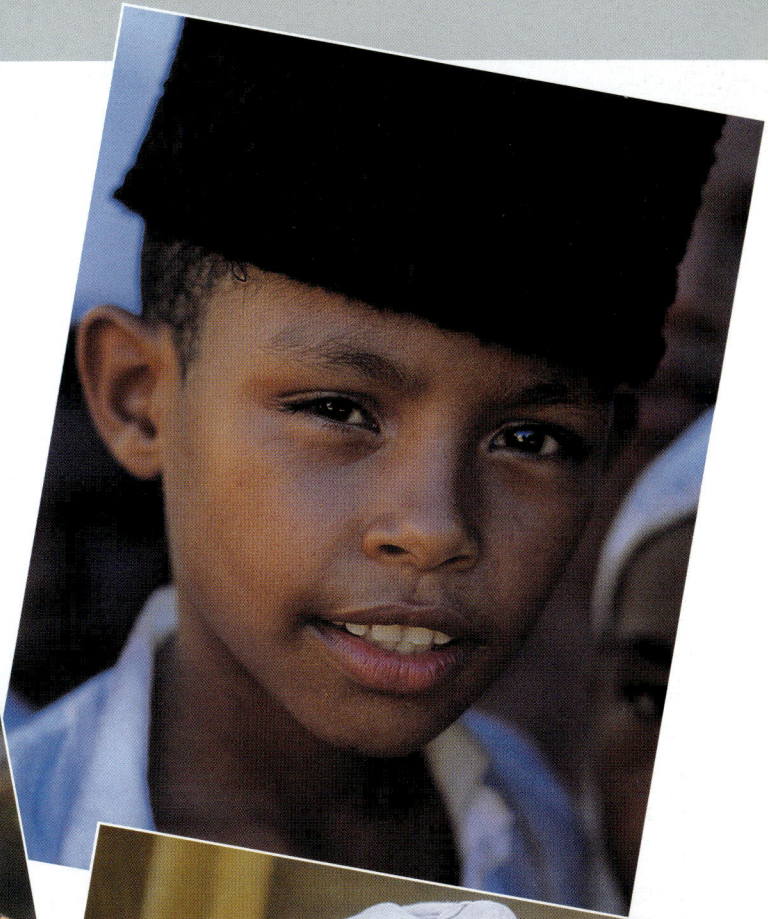

*RewindRewind*Rewind

What is the difference between founders such as Muhammad ﷺ and Guru Nanak Dev Ji and others such as Jesus?

29

In Arabic, Muslims call God – Allah.

Muhammad ﷺ was the founder of Islam and the Final Prophet. In their statement of belief Muslims say:

'an la ilaha illal lahu wa anna Muhammadar rasulul lahi'

'there is no god but Allah and Muhammad is the messenger of Allah'

It is very important to remember that, unlike Jesus, Muhammad ﷺ is not believed to be God. He was an ordinary human being who was chosen by God to receive God's message and to teach it to other people.

A page from an ancient Qur'an

Muslims never pray to Muhammad ﷺ but they show great respect towards him. The messages which Muhammad ﷺ received from God are written down in the Muslim holy book, the Qur'an, but Muslims also have the Hadith which contains stories about the life of Muhammad ﷺ and teachings which he gave to his followers. The Hadith has a special place in the life of Muslims as, when in doubt, they can look back to the example of the Prophet and see how he dealt with particular situations.

There are several stories about the birth of Muhammad ﷺ.

Muhammad ﷺ was born in 570 CE in Makkah which is now in Saudi Arabia. His mother was called Amina and his father, 'Abd Allah. 'Abd Allah died before Muhammad ﷺ was born. On the night that Amina gave birth to Muhammad ﷺ a large star appeared in the sky. The Prophet's grandfather, 'Abd al-Muttalib spent six days trying to think of a name for the baby boy. On the seventh day he had a dream and was told that the boy should be called Muhammad ﷺ which means 'The Praised One'. He rushed to tell Amina and discovered that she had had the same dream.

At that time it was the custom in Makkah to send young children from the city to the oasis at Taif, where there was plenty of good food. This enabled the children to grow up strong and healthy. Women from the desert came into Makkah to collect the young children and to receive money for looking after them. Because Amina was a widow she did not have enough money to pay for Muhammad ﷺ to go to Taif.

Finally, a poor woman called Halima agreed to take the boy. She had a son of the same age as Muhammad ﷺ. Halima was worried about how she was going to feed the two children because the land on her farm was very poor and grew very little. All she could do was to pray to Allah for help.

When she reached her farm she found that the fields were full of wheat and the trees were covered in fruit. She had three times as many goats as when she had left and the sheep and camels were producing milk again. Both boys grew to be strong and healthy and after three years she returned Muhammad ﷺ to Amina.

Three years later Amina took Muhammad ﷺ to Yathrib (now called Al-Madinah) to visit her relatives. When they started for home, however, Amina died and Muhammad ﷺ had to live with his grandfather 'Abd al-Muttalib. Two years later, when Muhammad ﷺ was eight, Abd al-Muttalib also died and the boy went to live with Abu Talib, his uncle.

text message.........

Remember: Muslims do not believe that Muhammad ﷺ is God. He was an ordinary human being who was chosen by God to receive God's message and to teach it to other people. Muslims never pray to Muhammad ﷺ but they show great respect towards him.

✋ STOP & Think ❓

➤ What other birth stories of religious leaders do you know about?

➤ Why do you think these stories are so important to believers?

➤ Why might some people say that Muhammad ﷺ had a very hard life as a

Abu Talib was a merchant and took Muhammad ﷺ with him on his journeys. One story tells how they were passing through Syria, near to the city of Busra, when his uncle was greeted by a monk called Bahira. The monk believed that one day a great prophet would arrive and hoped that he would live to see him.

Bahira had seen the camel train approaching and had noticed that a single cloud was travelling with them, just as though it was sheltering someone from the sun.

Bahira invited the merchants to a meal in his cell. Later he asked if they were all present in his cell. Abu Talib said that he had left Muhammad ﷺ to look after the camels. Bahira sent for him and asked him many questions.

Finally, he asked Muhammad ﷺ to swear by the idol gods of Makkah, al-Lat and al-Uzza. Muhammad ﷺ refused. Bahira spoke to Abu Talib and said: 'This child is will be a great leader. Take him back to your country and look after him well'.

Muhammad ﷺ continued to work for his uncle as a camel driver and soon gained the respect of everyone who met him. He was known as al-Amin, the trustworthy one. A wealthy widow, Khadijah heard about his honesty, and employed Muhammad ﷺ to look after her businesses. She was so impressed with him that she asked him to marry her although she was much older than him. Muhammad ﷺ and Khadijah were well suited to each other and were very happily married. Together they had six children: two sons and four daughters. The two sons both died in childhood, but the daughters survived and themselves were happily married.

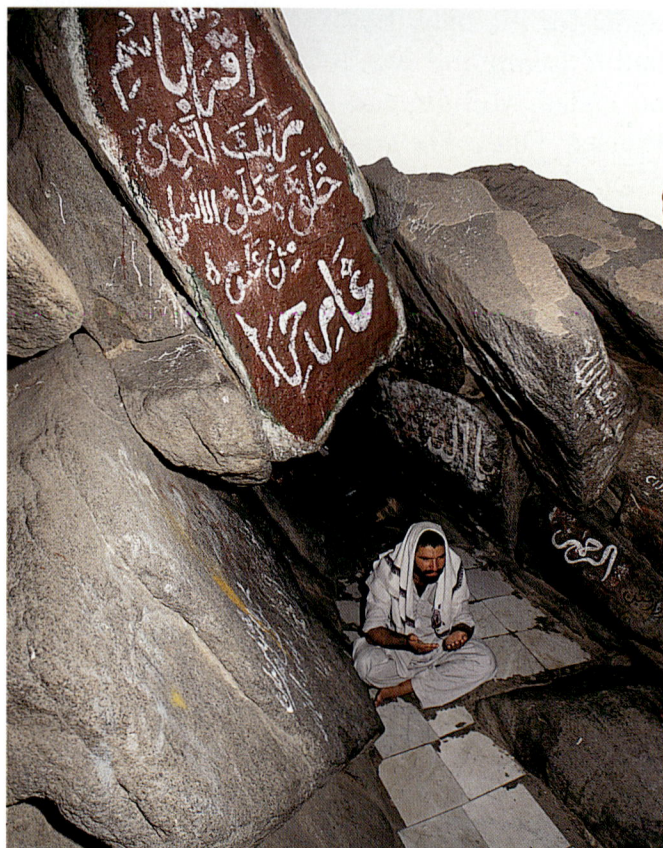

The cave on Mount Nur where Jibril spoke to Muhammad ﷺ.

Makkah was a busy trading centre and although many people worshipped idols in the Ka'bah, Muhammad ﷺ felt that they were not living their lives as God would have wanted. He liked to escape from the noise and bustle of life in the city by going into the hills or the desert to sit and pray. One night, in 611 CE, he was sitting in a cave on Mount Nur. He looked up and saw an enormous figure across the horizon. This was the Angel Jibril (Gabriel) who appeared before him and commanded him:

In the name
Of thy Lord and Cherisher,
Who created —

Created man, out of
A (mere) clot
Of congealed blood:

Proclaim!
And thy Lord
Is Most Bountiful —

He Who taught
(The use of) the Pen —
Taught man that
Which he knew not.'

(Surah 96 Al 'Alaq (The Clinging Clot) or Iqra' (Read!) 2-5

Then the angel said, 'O Muhammad ﷺ you are the messenger of Allah and I am Jibril'. Muhammad ﷺ could not read or write, so he had to repeat the words spoken to him until he could remember them. The figure that appeared to him was the Angel Jibril (Gabriel). Jibril told Muhammad ﷺ that he was to be the Messenger of Allah.

Not surprisingly, Muhammad ﷺ was terrified and ran home to his wife. She felt that he had really had a visit from Jibril and took Muhammad ﷺ to her cousin, a Christian called Waraqa who agreed that Muhammad ﷺ was the Prophet chosen for the Arabs who had been predicted in the Bible. This first night of revelations is called Laylat-ul Qard – the Night of Power.

The next revelation came to Muhammad ﷺ while he was resting at home one night. In this message he was ordered to tell the people of Makkah what he had learnt. Muhammad ﷺ spoke to his cousin 'Ali, his friends Abu Bakr and Uthman and a slave called Bilal (Zayd Bin Haritha) who had been given his freedom by Abu Bakr.

These five were the first Muslims and this small group met together to pray to Allah and faced Jerusalem in their prayers.

action INTO

❶ Find a map of the eastern Mediterranean.
  • Copy the map and mark on it the cities of Makkah and al-Madinah.
  • Find out where the main trade routes where and mark these on the map.
❷ Make a chart with two columns.
  • In the first column write down the important events in Muhammd's ﷺ life.
  • In the second column write down what you feel have been important events in your life.
  • Add further events to the chart as you learn more about Muhammad ﷺ.

text message.........

Bilal was the son of a Christian princess from Yemen. She was captured by the rulers of Makkah, and fell in love with an African slave called Riah. Bilal was their only child.
Bilal worked for an important man called Umaya. Bilal wanted to follow the teachings of Muhammad ﷺ but Umaya would not allow this.
Every day Bilal was taken out of Makkah at noon and made to lie on the sand under the burning sun with a stone on his chest. Bilal refused to give up his faith and eventually he was bought from Umaya by Abu Bakr.

The messages that Muhammad ﷺ received from Allah through Jibril continued for several years. Often they were very painful experiences for Muhammad ﷺ and he had violent fits.

At first, there were very few people who would listen to his messages. People in Makkah ridiculed Muhammad ﷺ and complained about his preaching. They were not prepared to change their way of worship and they were also concerned that they would lose money from people coming to worship the idols in the Ka'bah.

In 622 CE Khadijah died and so did Muhammad ﷺ's uncle Abu Talib. Muhammad ﷺ was by now very unpopular.

Muhammad leaves Makkah

The people of the city of Yathrib, 480km north east of Makkah, asked Muhammad ﷺ to go there as their governor. Already there were many Muslims living in Yathrib who had left Makkah because of the danger they were in.

Muhammad ﷺ was willing to go but could not leave Makkah in case he was seen by his enemies. The leaders of an important tribe, the Quraysh, were plotting against him and met to find a way of destroying Muhammad ﷺ. If any person was suspected of causing the death of the Prophet, they knew that Muhammad ﷺ's family would take revenge on them. One of the leaders, called Abu Jahl came up with a plan. One man from every group or tribe would wait outside Muhammad ﷺ's house all night and they would all kill him together when he came out in the morning.

That night Jibril appeared to Muhammad ﷺ and warned him not to sleep at home. The Prophet asked 'Ali to sleep in his house instead and promised that no harm would come to him. Next morning, the murderers where shocked when 'Ali opened the door and realised they had been tricked.

Muhammad ﷺ and Abu Bakr set off on two fast camels. They left Makkah, going south, in order to trick the people looking for him. Later they turned north towards Yathrib.

When they reached a mountain called Thawr, they stopped and hid in a cave. The Quraysh had already begun to search for Muhammad ﷺ. They were travelling across the desert and coming close to Thawr. Muhammad ﷺ and Abu Bhakr could hear them and stood very still. Muhammad ﷺ said that God would not let them be harmed.

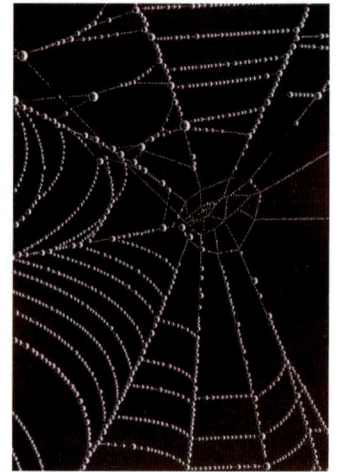

They could hear the men outside. One of them said, 'No one's been in this cave for a long time because there is a spider's web across the entrance and a dove nesting on the ledge'. Soon the men moved on and left the cave.

Abu Bakr could not understand, he had not seen the spider or the dove when they entered the cave but Muhammad ﷺ knew it was God's work.

After a few days, when they were sure that the Quraysh had left, they continued on their journey to Yathrib where Muhammad ﷺ was welcomed by the Muslims there. The city was renamed Madinah al-Nabi – City of the Prophet. Today it is known as al-Madinah.

The Hijrah

The Hijrah, or emigration, to Madinah is a very important event for Muslims and is placed at the beginning of the calendar as the first day of the first year of Islam. So the Muslim years are numbered 1 AH, 2 AH (after Hijrah) etc. The Hijrah is known as the birth of the Islamic community.

After Muhammad's ﷺ arrival, the very first mosque was built in al-Madinah. They now had to decide how they were going to call people to prayer. They wanted to avoid using any of the ways of other religions. One of Muhammad's ﷺ followers, Abdullah bin Zaid, said that he had had a dream in which he heard a human voice calling people to pray.

Muhammad ﷺ decided that this must be God's will so the next decision was who should be chosen to make the call. Muhammad ﷺ chose Bilal, saying that he had the best voice. Bilal then climbed on to the highest roof and gave the first call to prayer:

Allahu akbar

Allah is the Greatest

I bear witness that there is no god but Allah

I bear witness that Muhammad ﷺ is Allah's messenger

Rush to prayer

Rush to success

Allah is the greatest

There is no god but Allah

INTO action

❶ Try to find out as much as you can about Muhammad's ﷺ life. Use this book and any other information you can find.

❷ Prepare a list of questions which you could use to find out from a Muslim why Muhammad ﷺ was important and how his teachings and example continue to influence and guide them.

Use the answers from these questions to produce a table showing the response to each of the things you have asked.

STOP & Think

➤ Why did Muhammad ﷺ have to leave Makkah?

➤ How was he protected during his journey?

➤ Why do you think Muhammad ﷺ wanted the Call to Prayer to be different from that of other religions. Try to think of more than one reason.

Living in the new Muslim community at al-Madinah was not easy. There were many clans amongst the tribes and many battles. Muhammad ﷺ was called upon to negotiate the ending of many of these fights.

During this time Muhammad ﷺ received more revelations from Jibril and in one of these he learnt that Muslims should now pray facing the Ka'bah in Makkah.

In 624 CE Muhammad ﷺ led his followers into battle against soldiers from Makkah. They won and this victory established his authority both in politics and religion. All the Arabs became Muslims whilst the Jews in the area were allowed to continue in their own faith. However, they fought again in 627 at the battle of al-Khandaq – the trench. This ended with a treaty in 628 and Muslims were free to travel again to visit the Ka'bah in Makkah.

The first Hajj

Muhammad ﷺ led the first pilgrimage to Makkah in 630. Again there was a threat of fighting from some Makkans but Muhammad ﷺ instructed everyone to stay indoors when his army entered the city. Although there was some fighting Makkah eventually surrendered to Muhammad's ﷺ army.

As soon as they had entered Makkah, Muhammad ﷺ went straight to the Ka'bah. He rode around it seven times, destroyed all the idols which were inside and then cleaned it.

This event was the first Hajj – the annual pilgrimage to Makkah, which is one of the Five Pillars of Islam that all Muslims try to obey. At the end of this first Hajj, Muhammad ﷺ preached a sermon on Mount Arafat.

Muslim pilgrims pray towards the Ka'bah (the cube-shaped structure) in the centre of the Gand Mosque in Makkah.

In this sermon he told the Muslims how they should behave:

- He said that everyone's property was their own and stealing was always wrong.

- No one was allowed to charge interest on lending money.

- Husbands and wives must treat their partners with respect.

- No Muslim is better than any other Muslim.

- Muslims should follow the teachings of the Qur'an and the example of Muhammad ﷺ.

- People would be judged by Allah to see how well they lived.

- They should worship Allah, pray, fast during the month of Ramadan and pay Zakah (an annual payment to the community).

- Look after their servants and feed them and clothe them well.

- There would be no more prophets after Muhammad ﷺ.

On the same day, Muhammad ﷺ received his last revelation from Jibril:

'This day have I
Perfected your religion
For you, completed
My favour upon you,
And have chosen for you
Islam as your religion.'
Surah 5 Al Ma'idah (The Repast) 3

Muhammad ﷺ died in al-Madinah on 12th Rabi' ul-Awwal (8 June) in 632. When he died, Bilal was so distressed that he could not stand and so, for the first time, could not give the call to prayer.

After his death Abu Bakr came out to speak to the crowd:

'Surely he who worshipped Muhammad ﷺ should know that Muhammad ﷺ is dead, but he who worshipped Allah should know that Allah is alive and never dies.'

text message.........

Remember: Muslims believe that Muhammad ﷺ was a prophet, a messenger from Allah. This is different from Christians who believe that Jesus was actually God.
Abu Bakr made this clear to the Muslims when Muhammad ﷺ died:
'Surely he who worshipped Muhammad ﷺ should know that Muhammad ﷺ is dead, but he who worshipped Allah should know that Allah is alive and never dies.'

RewindRewindRewind

- What examples did Muhammad ﷺ say that Muslims should follow?

- What did Muhammad ﷺ say about borrowing money?

- What did Muhammad ﷺ say about how Muslims should treat other people?

Islam is the second largest of the world religions and also the fastest growing of them. It is estimated that there are more than eight hundred million Muslims in the world today. Although the religion of Islam began in the country now known as Saudi Arabia there are now Muslims living in every country.

The word 'Islam' means 'submission'. Muslims are people who submit themselves, or follow the will of Allah.

Muhammad ﷺ was the founder of Islam, a new religion. Muslims see him as the last in a line of prophets which begin with Adam. Most of the prophets of Islam are found in the Torah – the Jewish Scriptures (and the Old Testament of the Christian Bible) as well as in the Qur'an. This is because Islam teaches that God tried to teach his people how they should behave and live a religious life three times. The first time was to the Jews and then, later, he sent Jesus. However, each time, people changed the message that they had received from God and it became corrupted. Muhammad ﷺ was the last of the prophets and there would be no more.

Muslims believe that the Qur'an is the direct word of Allah revealed to Muhammad ﷺ by Jibril. No word of the Qur'an has been changed since Muhammad ﷺ received it and the Qur'an on earth is just a copy of the real Qur'an which is in heaven.

Muslims lead their lives following the teachings of God in the Qur'an and also by learning from the teachings and life of Muhammad ﷺ which are found in the Hadith.

As well as receiving the Qur'an, Muhammad ﷺ brought peace amongst the many fighting tribes of Arabia. He cleansed the Ka'bah and removed the idols in it and established Makkah as a holy city for all Muslims.

As well as Makkah, al-Madinah – where the first mosque was built, and Jerusalem are also holy cities. One night, shortly before Muhammad ﷺ left Makkah for al-Madinah, he travelled with Jibril, on a winged animal called Buraq, from Makkah to Jerusalem and then on through the seven heavens. The is remembered by Muslims as Laylat ul Isra wal Mi'raj.

The Five Pillars of Islam

The way of life which Muhammad ﷺ gave to his followers can be found in the Five Pillars of Islam.

As part of their submission to the will of Allah, Muslims follow the Five Pillars which are visible signs of their way of life and the unity of the ummah, the worldwide Muslim community:

- **Shahadah** – the declaration of faith – 'There is no god but Allah; Muhammad ﷺ is the messenger of Allah'.

- **Salah** – Compulsory prayers five times a day.

- **Zakah** – Purification of wealth by payment of annual welfare due. Muslims give 2.5% of their surplus income every year. It helps the Ummah (community of Muslims) and is shared for the benefit of everyone. It helps the people who give because they know that they are not being greedy or selfish with their money.

- **Hajj** – the Pilgrimage to Makkah made during the Muslim month of Dhul-Hijjah. This is a duty which every Muslim tries to carry out once in their lifetime.

- **Sawm** – this is fasting during the hours of daylight for the whole of the month of Ramadan. This helps Muslims to focus on prayer and the Qur'an, to know that they are obeying God and to share the experience with the rest of the worldwide community of Muslims.

THE FIVE PILLARS

SHAHADAH SALAH ZAKAH SAWM HAJJ

The Five Pillars of Islam

text message.........

All Muslims should live their lives in submission to the will of Allah.
All Muslims should follow the Five Pillars: Shahadah, Salah, Zakah, Hajj, Sawm.

RewindRewind**Rewind**

- Where do Muslims say the real Qur'an is?
- What is Sawm?
- What are the three holy cities of Islam and why are they important?

What do you know?

❶ Where was Muhammad ﷺ born?

❷ What does this symbol mean: ﷺ?

❸ Who was Muhammad's ﷺ first wife?

❹ Who gave the first part of the Qur'an to Muhammad ﷺ and where did this happen?

❺ Who was Bahira and what did he do?

❻ Write a paragraph about Bilal.

❼ Why did Muhammad ﷺ go to Yathrib – al-Madinah?

❽ What did Muhammad ﷺ do at the Ka'bah in 630?

❾ Where did Muhammad ﷺ give his last sermon?

❿ What are the Five Pillars?

What do you think?

❶ Muslims do not allow pictures of people, including Muhammad ﷺ. They say that pictures like this would be disrespectful to Allah. Can you think why they say this?

❷ From what you have read, what sort of person do you think Muhammad ﷺ was?

❸ Think about the rules which Muhammad ﷺ gave his followers in his last sermon. Explain why each of these are important for Muslims.

❹ Why do you think Allah chose Muhammad ﷺ to be his messenger?

In the mosques decorative geometric patterns are used rather than statues or pictures.

action INTO

❶ Take each of the Five Pillars and explain how Muslims perform them and why they are important.

❷ Make a chart about founders. You can choose founders of different religions as well as those of charities, schools or other organisations. For each one, except Muhammad ﷺ, try to find a picture of the founder.

❸ Islamic patterns like the one on page 40 are made up from many different geometric shapes like triangles, squares and kites. Using squared paper, design your own pattern and remember not to draw animals or people.

❹ Write a short article in which a Muslim explains why Muhammad ﷺ is so important to them.

❺ Write a prayer which includes thanking God for life and creation, asking God to look after people who are suffering and also ask for help in living a better life.

Final Thoughts

In this unit you have learnt about Muhammad ﷺ the founder of one of the world's religions.

What have you learnt about Muhammad's ﷺ life and how he came to be the Prophet of Islam?

Explain how Muhammad's ﷺ example might be a good guide for all people today.

How do you think that a strong religious belief might help someone to live a better life and be happier?

WHO WAS GOTAMA BUDDHA?

Each year millions of people go to visit sights connected with a man who lived over two and a half thousand years ago.

Why was he important?

Why do so many people believe he gave a message for all time?

The Temple of the Reclining Buddha – Bangkok, Thailand

Tooth Relic Temple – Kandy, Sri Lanka

Dambula Rock Cave – Sri Lanka

The Temple of the
Emerald Buddha –
Bangkok, Thailand

Angkor Wat –
Cambodia

Where and when was Gotama Buddha born?

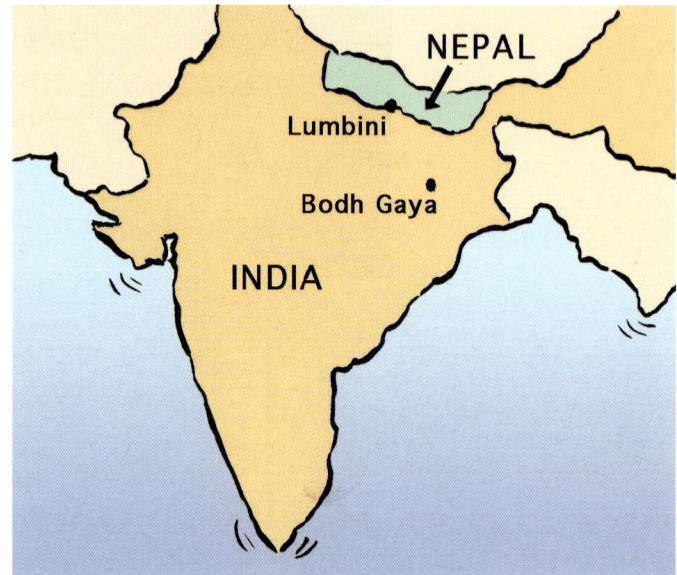

STOP & Think

➤ How can you tell the person in the picture is special?

➤ What sort of mood do you think he is expressing?

➤ What evidence do you have for your answers?

The Big Picture

In this unit you will learn:

• Where and when Gotama Buddha was born

• Why he decided to leave home

• How he became enlightened

• What his main teachings were

• The importance of his life and teachings for people today.

A prince called Siddattha

Just across the Indian border, at the foot of the Himalayan mountains in Nepal, is the village of Lumbrini. It was here, two and a half thousand years ago, that Siddattha Gotama was born. Gotama was the family name into which he was born. The title Buddha was to come much later in the story of his life.

His father was a rich and important ruler. His mother was Queen Mayadevi and she had had a dream that her child would become a pure and powerful being. When Gotama was born, it is said that the gods Brahma and Indra took the baby painlessly from the Queen's side.

The king named the baby Siddattha, meaning wish-fulfilled, and he asked a wise Hindu priest to foretell the baby's future. The priest predicted that Siddattha would either become a ruler of the entire world or he would be a holy man who would search for the true meaning of life. The king wanted his son to be a great ruler of people just like himself.

A life of luxury

The king loved his son and was worried for his future. He thought the best way to protect him would be to keep him within the palace's large grounds so that he would never see anything to make him unhappy or know about suffering in the outside world. So he was brought up in luxury surrounded by beautiful things, not wanting for anything. He never went beyond the palace walls so he had no idea of how different life was outside. If one of the palace workers became sick then the King ordered them not to work. In this way Siddattha would not know that people could become ill. Similarly, only young and beautiful people would be around him so he knew nothing of what happened when people became old.

STOP & Think

➤ Why did Siddattha's father try and protect his son from all the sufferings in the world?

➤ Do you think having lots of money and luxuries make people happy?

➤ What else might be needed?

Learning to be a ruler

Siddattha grew up, following in his father's footsteps. He became good at many things including sport and art. A beautiful princess was chosen to be his wife. Her name was Yasodhara and they had a son called Rahula. The king continued to make sure that Siddattha wanted for nothing and although Siddattha was now a young man, he still knew nothing about life in the world outside the royal palaces.

PAUSE & RECORD

• Write a list of what Prince Siddattha would not have seen or experienced by having to stay within the castle walls.

• Was the king kind or cruel for trying to keep Siddattha protected?

Give one reason for each point of view.

45

In spite of everything that was done to make him happy, Siddattha began to grow more and more restless. He was curious to see for himself what was beyond the palace walls. So eventually he persuaded his father to let him go into the outside world. For the first time in his life he was going to be taken by chariot through the city.

Imagine! Here was Prince Siddattha, a grown up, asking questions like a child. He just couldn't believe his eyes. Everything seemed so new to him on the streets. He asked his charioteer, Chanda, question upon question. Chanda had known the Prince since he was a baby. He didn't want to hurt him or make him distressed but he did think it was only fair to tell him the truth.

There were four sights that really made Siddattha stop and think:

A very old and frail person

A person suffering in great pain through illness

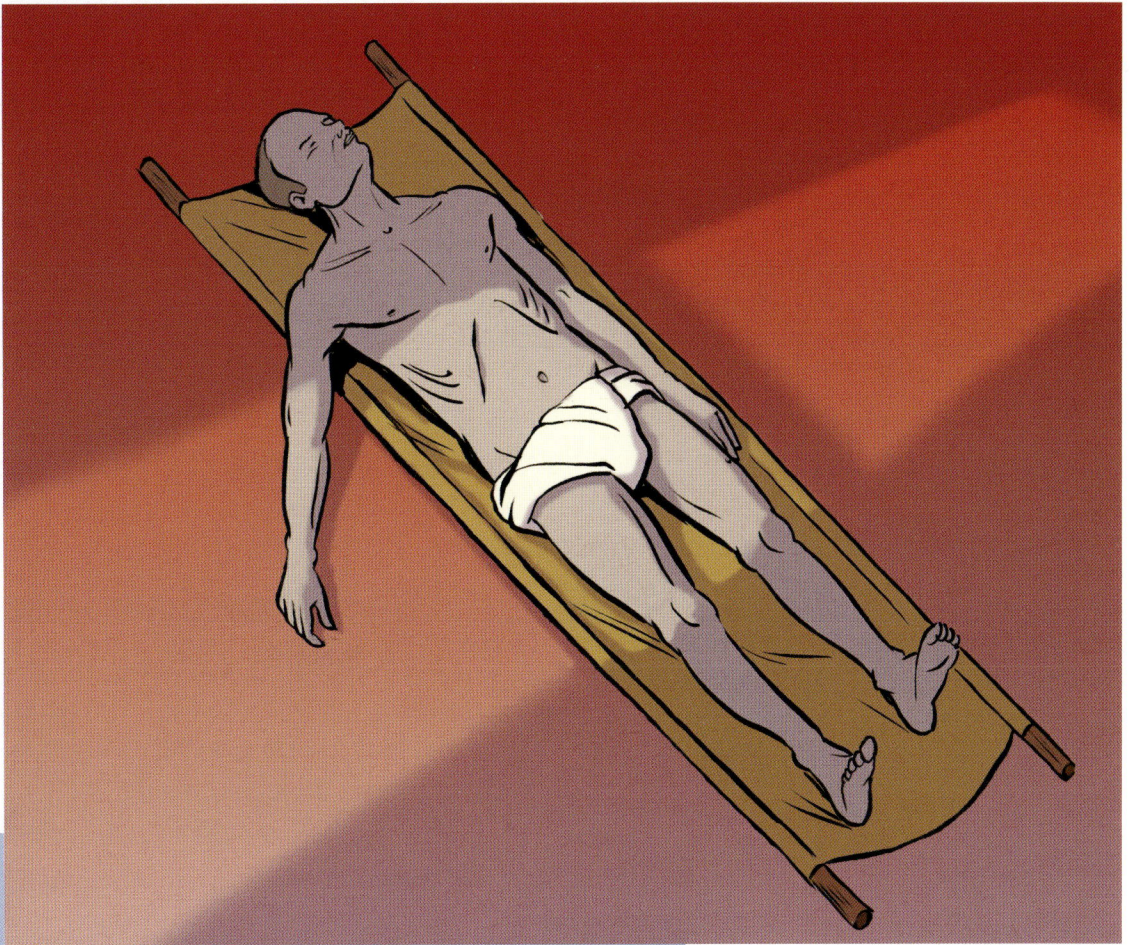

A dead body

A holy man

The journey that changed everything

SIDDATTHA: Don't go so fast, Chanda. There's so much to take in. It feels like being in a foreign country.

CHANDA: Your father would not be pleased if we were late, Master.

SIDDATTHA: But there's so much to see. These are my father's people. If I'm going to be ruler of them one day I want to see them and be among them.

CHANDA: But it is not necessary for you to be so close to them. Your father loves you dearly and wants to protect you from anything unpleasant. He wouldn't want you to be worried or upset by anything.

SIDDATTHA: Stop Chanda! There is someone lying down over there. He is clutching his stomach and crying out. What is the matter with him?

CHANDA: He is obviously ill, Master. Everyone becomes ill at some time in their life.

SIDDATTHA: But why? What does it mean?

CHANDA: The body is not able to stand up to all the strains and stresses of life in this world. It can become injured or diseased. This can cause pain and discomfort.

SIDDATTHA: I should have known this. I should have been told.

STOP & Think ?

➤ Select one other sight and write a play script of the questions Siddattha may have asked and how Chanda the charioteer replied to them.

➤ Have you ever had to explain something difficult to someone?

We all have times in our lives when we realise things for the first time

Innocent people often suffer.

So there is no Father Christmas.

Some people don't have beds.

Life could never be the same again

After what he had seen, Siddattha could never again view the world in the same way. He couldn't just put what he had seen to the back of his mind and forget about it. He felt he needed to try and find some answers to the true meaning of life and why there was suffering. He knew he would never do this by separating himself from the world in his rich and comfortable palace.

So, taking off his expensive clothes and jewellery, and leaving behind his family and home comforts, he set out for a new life.

He looked for the truth in many different ways. He had discussions with groups. He consulted with holy men. He went to great extremes, including going without food for long periods of time. Years went by and still he had not found the answers he was looking for. Finally, weary from his travels he decided not to move until he had found the answer. He sat under a tree to meditate.

The word for enlightenment is 'bodhi' which is why the tree he sat under became known as the Bodhi Tree. The things he now saw and understood clearly became the teachings which Buddhists follow today.

text message.........

Meditation means thinking very deeply and carefully. In order to do this, a person has to shut out all other thoughts so they are able to fully concentrate and not be distracted. To reach this state of mind, many people begin by practising breathing in a particular calm and rhythmic way. They may use a picture, symbol or object such as a flower on which to focus their attention. They may sit in a special way that is relaxed and comfortable. Many find that meditation helps the things they have been puzzling over to become clearer in their minds. They also find it can help them to cope with problems they may be having. It makes them feel stronger and ready to face up to their difficulties.

STOP & Think

➤ Where do you like to sit and think about important things?

➤ Think of three questions you might never know the answer to?

PAUSE & RECORD

• Write down ten people who adopt a title after achieving something, e.g. Prime Minister, Hajji.

• Can you think of five other words that are hard to explain? Choose one of them and try to make its meaning clear. You might like to use a simile (comparing it with something else) or an illustration.

Siddattha 'sees the light'

As Siddattha meditated he began to realise certain things about the world. He became awake to the truth about what causes suffering and what stops it. This 'awakening' is called **enlightenment**. From that time, Siddattha became known as the Buddha which means 'the Awakened One' or 'The Enlightened One.'

Are you telling me the truth?

text message.........

Enlightenment is not an easy word to explain. It has been described as being set free from the things that hinder you from understanding the truth. It is when people suddenly see things in a different way - like a mist clearing - and realise something for the first time. Although Buddhists believe that everyone can eventually achieve enlightenment, they describe Siddhattha as the Buddha because they believe he was the first to have become enlightened in this way.

Is it true the tooth fairy will come?

I will always be true to you.

PAUSE & RECORD

- Add two more important truths about life that you believe in?
- Give your reasons for their importance to you

These are the truths we learn from his teachings.

Nothing stays the same

We have learned that the Buddha understood the truth of certain things. What does this mean? We use the word **truth** in many different ways.

The kind of truths which the Buddha taught are about important aspects of life and its meaning rather than mere everyday facts.

One important truth that came to Siddattha was that everything in the world is constantly changing. Nothing lasts forever. Until people can accept this, they will always suffer.

PAUSE & RECORD

- What other examples can you think of that show how things change?
- Which changes are you looking forward to in your own life and which ones are you not looking forward to?

After his long period of meditation, the Buddha went on to explain the truths he had discovered about change and suffering at his first sermon. This happened at a place known as Sanarth near Banares. The teaching he gave is known as **The Four Noble Truths.**

The Four Noble Truths

1. All life involves suffering

The Buddhist word for suffering is **dukkha**. It includes both physical and mental pain, covering everything from the pain of a headache to the deepest feelings of despair. The Buddha taught that even the happiest time has sadness attached to it, as we know it can't last.

Tomorrow is the last day. I can't bear the thought we've got to leave this fabulous place.

2. Suffering comes from desire

Usually, the reason why we suffer is because we crave or desire things that we haven't got or cannot have. This means we are never satisfied and we become frustrated and discontented.

If I had loads of money I could dress like that.

3. When craving stops, suffering will cease

If we learn to stop craving, we learn peace and contentment. Also, it is seen that the evil in the world is brought on by greed and envy. This causes others to suffer.

I don't care about that woman I just want the money.

4. Happiness comes through following The Middle Way

The Buddha had known the extremes of both a rich and poor way of life. He believed that neither was right and he set out eight steps which needed to be taken for a balanced life of 'The Middle Way'. These steps became known as 'The Eight-Fold Path'.

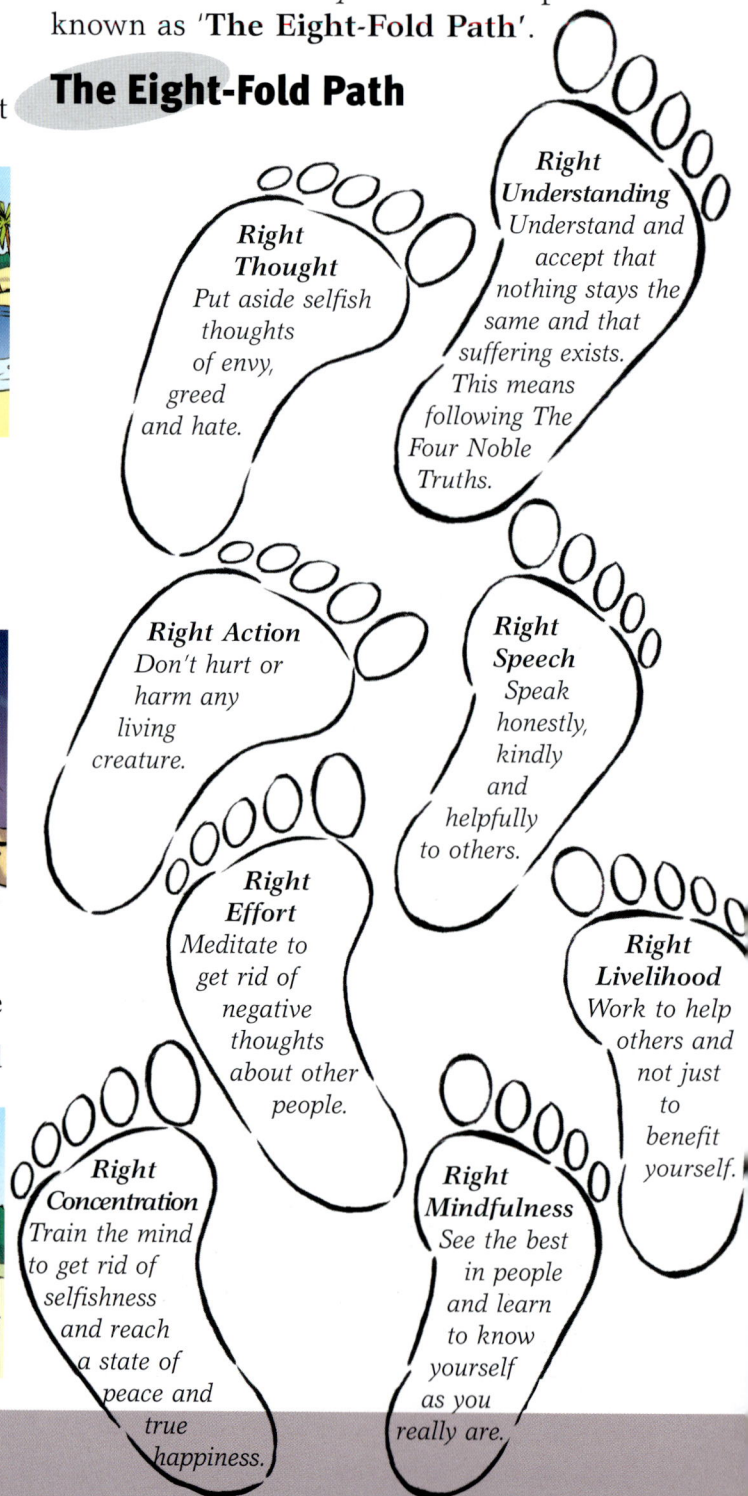

The Eight-Fold Path

Right Thought
Put aside selfish thoughts of envy, greed and hate.

Right Understanding
Understand and accept that nothing stays the same and that suffering exists. This means following The Four Noble Truths.

Right Action
Don't hurt or harm any living creature.

Right Speech
Speak honestly, kindly and helpfully to others.

Right Effort
Meditate to get rid of negative thoughts about other people.

Right Livelihood
Work to help others and not just to benefit yourself.

Right Concentration
Train the mind to get rid of selfishness and reach a state of peace and true happiness.

Right Mindfulness
See the best in people and learn to know yourself as you really are.

Buddhists do not consider the Buddha as a God but as someone who was a great teacher and guide. They see him as a role model for how to live their lives. Many of us have people we look up to and whose example we may try to follow. Sometimes they are people who have lived in the past and we have read or been told about them. Or they may be people we know who are living today.

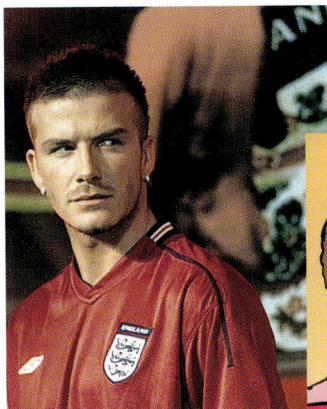

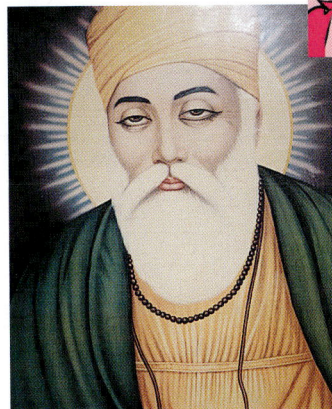

PAUSE & RECORD

- Have you ever felt envy?
- How has it made you feel? Try to draw an illustration of your feelings.
- How have you dealt with it?

text message........

Buddhists believe that if they follow the eight steps they will become enlightened and reach a state of mind, which they call Nirvana. Nirvana means 'blowing out' and it is thought that by being able to 'blow out' or extinguish all the feelings of envy and hate, they will see the world in a different way. They will be able to say they have reached Nirvana, a state of being content and at peace.

STOP & Think

➤ Who are the people who teach and guide you?

➤ Do you have people you would call a role model?

➤ In what way do you try and follow their example?

Buddhists show their respect for the Buddha in many ways

A Buddhist shrine where Buddhists can meditate upon the life and teachings of the Buddha.

Long after the Buddha died, his teachings were written down by his followers. Many Buddhists today like to study them.

Mount Kailas, Western Tibet. A place where Buddhists like to make a special journey to help them feel closer to his life and teachings.

*Monks in Ajanta caves in Maharashtra, India. After a long life of travelling and teaching, the Buddha died in Kushinara in northern India. His body was cremated and his ashes were given to different rulers. Special monuments called **stupas** were built over his remains. Today Buddhists visit them and pay their respects to his memory.*

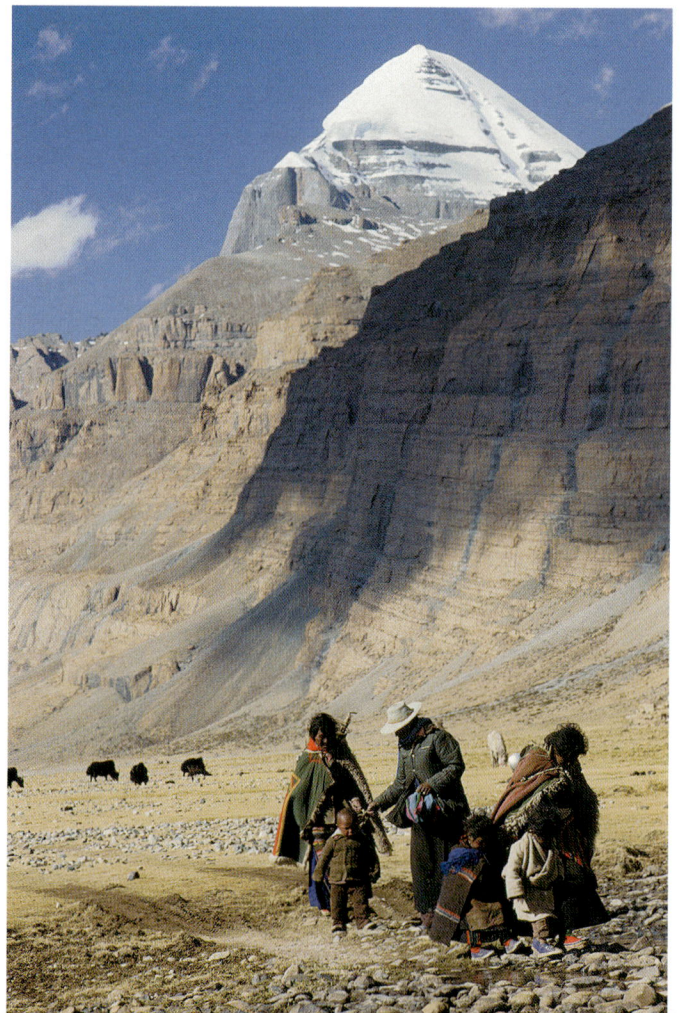

Buddhists in the 21st Century try to live as the Buddha taught

Buddhist monks protesting for peace.

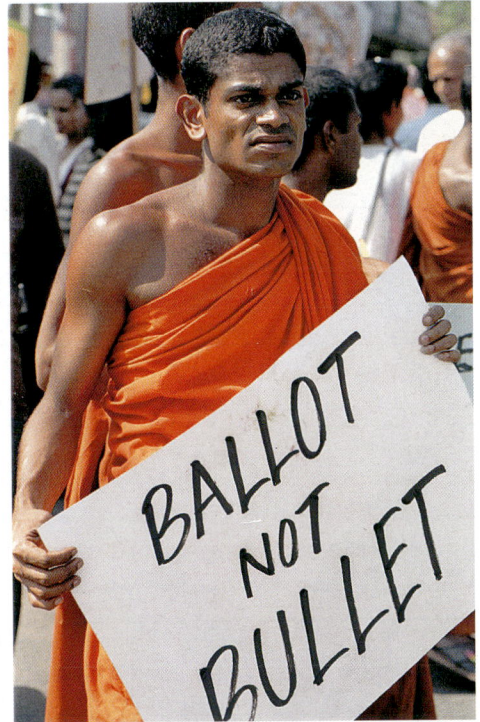

Buddhists belief in not harming any living creature means that they are vegetarians.

Showing compassion and giving guidance to those in prison.

STOP & Think

➤ What other special journeys do you know about where people go to show respect?

➤ Do you have a special symbol or object to remind you of someone important to you?

PAUSE & RECORD

• Study all the pictures on these pages carefully and write down any questions you would like to ask about them.

What do you know?

Using pages 41–55 to help you, work through the following questions and activities:

❶ In this unit, you have been introduced to many new words. Copy the table below into your books and write out the definitions in your own words.

Truth	
Meditation	
Dukkha	
Enlightenment	

❷ Look at the time-line below. There were many important events that happened in the life of the Buddha. Choose four important events in the life of the Buddha and place them along the time-line in the order in which you think they happened.

birth   death

❸ Underneath the time-line, copy out the events you have chosen. By each event, write a word describing an emotion you think Siddattha must have felt at that time. You need to explain why you think he felt this way and illustrate it with an appropriate illustration. The first example is done for you.

Seeing **The Four Sights** – *I think Siddattha must have felt* **confused** *because he had not realised that illness, death or old age existed. When he saw the holy man it would make him question what is really important in life.*

❹ Look at the following table. For each line you need to explain the connection between the three words.

Prince Siddattha ⟶	Gotama Buddha ⟶	The Buddha
Meditation ⟶	Enlightenment ⟶	Nirvana
The Middle way ⟶	The Four Noble Truths ⟶	The Eight-Fold Path

action INTO

❶ Write a letter from Siddattha to his father, explaining how you feel and why you have decided to leave home.

❷ Draw two eight-spoke wheels. In the first one describe something in each spoke that changed the life of the Buddha. In the second wheel, describe eight things that have changed in your own life.

❸ Make a collage from newspapers and magazines. On one side, use examples which show greed, hate and envy. On the other side, use images of peace and contentment. Add drawings and photos of your own if you wish.

❹ Using the information in this unit and the website www.buddhanet.net/ devise a tourist poster encouraging people to visit important places in the life of the Buddha. By each place you will need to explain why it is important for Buddhists today.

❺ Write a poem called: 'Nothing stays the same'.

What do you think?

❶ Imagine you could ask the Buddha two questions before his enlightenment and two questions after, what would you like to know the answer to?

❷ There are many different types of suffering in the world. Look at the picture on p6 and the picture of the rainforest being destroyed on p62. They which show two different kinds of disasters which cause suffering. Now explain what you think is an important difference between them.

❸ What answer do you think the Buddha might have given as to why there are these two examples of suffering?

Final thoughts

This unit has asked the question: Who was Gotama Buddha? You have learned that he discovered some important truths about life which he passed on to others. His discovery of these things is known as The Enlightenment. How enlightened do you feel about what you have learned? Write the word **Enlightenment** in the centre of a page in your book and around it write what important things you have come to understand and any questions that you would still like to find answers to.

Samantha's life began in the cool clear waters of a shallow river far from the sea. Soon after hatching she raised her head to see the sun, shimmering through the ripples of the water. Around her, millions of other salmon hatched, each enjoying these happy moments before their mighty swim to the great ocean. Samantha heard the sea calling her, just as it had her mother. She swam with the river, it flowed wider every moment, changing from a tiny gurgling stream to a powerful force, great hulking ships afloat above her head. Reaching the open oceans she swam with new creatures, strange, fearsome... every turn she took, another danger was there, another beautiful sight waiting.

Years passed and now she felt the call of the stream. She had to return. Just like her mother. She couldn't resist.

So she swam again, towards the river. This time against the flow. It was a struggle. Many times she wanted to give up, she knew she had to return, to create her own young. On she swam, exhausted. The wake of the mighty ships now dragged her down but on she swam. Suddenly her way was blocked. Concrete from the floor of the river, reaching into the sky. Blocking out the sun. She leapt towards the concrete wall, but couldn't get past. There was no way over or under. Exhausted, Samantha closed her eyes. She felt the riverbed brush her belly, and she flopped onto her side. Her journey was over... no young would come from her.

Up above, the workers on the dam set the turbines for another day.

Dam!

Every time a dam is built there are winners and losers:

- There's work for the local community
- The electricity produced by the dam can make people's lives easier
- People get rich from the designing, building and maintenance of the dam
- Scenic areas may be destroyed
- Wildlife habitat can be harmed
- People may have to move away from their homes as their land is flooded
- Traditional ways of working might have to change

STOP & Think

➤ **Which of the points above describe winners/losers?**

The Big Issues

What problems have scientists warned about?

Climate Change

The Greenhouse Effect is the theory that the earth's atmosphere is trapping more of the sun's rays and so warming the planet up. If temperatures rise only a little, this could change many things:

* More freak weather
* Rises in sea-level
* Changes to the pattern of food production.

All of these could have serious effects for life on earth. Climate change may be caused by:

The burning of **fossil fuels** like coal and oil.

The use of certain chemicals like **CFCs**.

Methane caused by cows passing gas and decomposing waste.

These can all lead to the production of **greenhouse gases** which 'trap' more of the sun's energy and warm up the planet.

Resource Depletion

The earth has only so many natural resources. These are **finite**. If not used wisely, they will eventually run out.

* We use natural resources for **energy**, like oil and gas. These will eventually run out. We also use other natural resources like ores and minerals. Supplies of these are limited.

* Some resources, like wood, are **renewable** but need time to recover.

* Life on earth is very varied. This **biodiversity** is important for the health of the planet. If we over-exploit it, we'll lose it. For example, many species are **endangered**. Once they're gone we can't bring them back.

We need to learn to use resources in a **sustainable** way.

Pollution

Everything we do causes pollution. From using cars, to our morning business down the toilet, all has its effect. Environmentalists believe that we should try to end **unnecessary** pollution.

Ralph Archibald is a garden gnome. He's made out of plaster. This was mined from deep inside the earth (where a forest used to be) then transported to factories by lorries belching fumes (causing lung problems for many). Lots of strange chemicals were added to bind him together (causing some pollution along the way). Then he was baked in an oven using vast amounts of gas (more energy, more greenhouse gases). Then paints made from oils and chemicals were added. He was transported to the garden centre by more lorries (cough, cough). Then he found a nice home. Unfortunately someone knocked him over at a barbecue. Never mind, he can easily be replaced...

Your Choice

Every time we buy product X instead of product Y we make a choice. Many believe that we should think about the environment when we are deciding what to buy. If something is good for the environment we call it 'environmentally-friendly' How often do we choose the environmentally friendly option? Why should we?

Here are three sponges. Which one would you buy?

This is made from the by-products of oil and other chemicals.

This is harvested from the sea and is then bleached to make it look clean.

This is harvested from the sea and is unbleached.

STOP & Think ?

➤ Which of the sponges is the most environmentally friendly option? (Look at the top of the next page for some comments after your discussion.)

PETROL CRISIS?

Britain 2000 – The country was almost brought to a halt by a blockade of petrol refineries by truckers unhappy about the rising cost of fuel. Petrol tanker drivers sometimes refused to cross the blockades. Petrol shortages caused many problems. The government reduced the taxation on petrol and so lowered its cost.

'We were right' – people need fuel to do their work. It's unfair that it costs so much in Britain. High fuel costs won't stop people using their cars. Public transport is so useless, we need cars.

'You were wrong' – people use too much fuel causing greenhouse gases; the only way to stop this is to put up the price. Life would be more pleasant and safer if fewer people used their cars. Why attack the government when it's trying to do its best for the environment?

Sponges: The unbleached natural sponge is probably best. The bleach used pollutes the sea. The synthetic one uses a lot of energy to make and uses chemicals which might get into natural systems and cause pollution. But, the unbleached one is still harvested from nature, and this is only good if that's done carefully and doesn't harm other creatures. See the difficulties in deciding what's best?

action INTO

You're about to buy a fridge. In groups, put the following list of requirements into order: 1 = most important, 10 = least important. Be honest and explain your views.

- The fridge looks nice.
- It uses a very small amount of energy.
- It is big and so can hold a lot of food.
- It has fancy gadgets for making special ice shapes.
- It uses chemicals which are good for the environment.
- It isn't expensive.
- It is very trendy.
- It is easy to keep clean.
- It has a built-in ice-cream maker.
- It is very quiet.

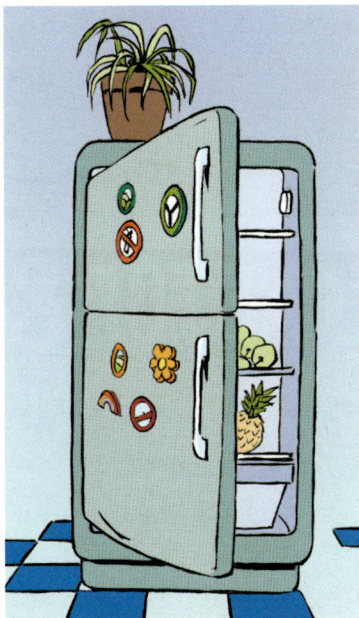

text message.........

Most bins are collected once a week. The average amount of weekly family rubbish weighs about 10kg. Most of this is some kind of plastic. Plastic is very difficult to dispose of if it isn't recycled. If it is buried or burned it can give off dangerous chemicals which can find their way into the foods we eat and air we breathe. Most plastic is used only to transport goods from the shop to your house.

❙❙ PAUSE & RECORD

- Find two newspaper stories about environmental problems. One story should be local and the other global. Write your own view on the issue

Laurence is in prison. He's locked up 24 hours a day. He will never see his family again, and never go home. He can't choose what food he has or when he has it. His whole world is his cage. His crime? None. He's a lion in a zoo.

Sally has what seems like a cold. It's made her weak. She'll take a long time to recover. But she won't. She's to be killed, along with all her friends, and even those who live a mile away in every direction. Her body will be added to the pile and burned. Sally is a sheep. They think she has foot & mouth disease.

Oliver has been in the same place for 300 years. He's quite happy. He provides a home for thousands of living things. He helps keep the air fresh and is beautiful to look at. Throughout his life he's brought happiness to many generations and sweet memories of childhood for those now grown old. Oliver's an oak tree. He's in the way of the new motorway. He's about to be cut down.

Human Responsibility

When it comes to nature, humans seem a bit confused. We've got dolphin friendly tuna but not tuna friendly tuna. We seem to treat nature in ways we don't treat each other:

- we don't eat people
- we don't carry out experiments on people without their permission
- we don't destroy people when they are in our way
- we don't decide that some people's lives are worth living and others aren't.

But we seem to do all of these things to other forms of life on earth.

Do we treat life on earth just as it suits us?

✋ STOP & Think 💡

➤ Does the environment have any rights? What are they?

➤ How do you feel about Laurence, Sally and Oliver? Explain why.

Why care for the environment?

Some people believe that humans should look after the environment. This is because we're the most powerful living thing on earth. We can think about the future and plan for it, whereas most other living things live for the moment.

Some think we should show good **stewardship** of nature. This means that we look after it today in a way which makes sure it'll still be there tomorrow (and for many years to come). This could mean that we have to treat all life on earth as if it is valuable – and realise that human needs and wants aren't the only important things in life.

Perhaps we should care for nature because:

- Nature has rights just like us, because other living things have the right to be themselves. This is called the *intrinsic value* of the environment.

- If we don't treat nature properly, then maybe we'll pay the price later. Badly treating the environment might make human life harder in future. This is called the *instrumental value* of the environment. Life on earth is finely balanced. One thing sometimes depends a lot on another. This is called **interdependence**.

But, many people seem to put their own needs and wants first, and not think too much about how their actions might affect the environment.

CASE STUDY: THE CAR

Someone once suggested that the car was the biggest danger to the environment ever invented.

I don't like cars because they kill people. Around 250,000 people die every year in car accidents, not to mention countless other life-forms killed by cars. There are around 680 million cars on the planet. They use about half the oil produced in the world, and are major causes of pollution. Vast amounts of land are used for roads and parking. They needlessly destroy the environment.

I like cars because they give me freedom. They've improved a lot over the years and so don't pollute as much as they used to. Cars aren't dangerous, but some people who drive them are. Buses and trains use fuel and cause pollution too, and as for aeroplanes, they're the worst. Even if everyone travelled by bicycle there'd still be pollution and accidents. We should improve cars so they're better for the environment, not ban them – get real. Fancy cycling when you're 90 eh?

action INTO

Have a class debate: "Cars should be banned except for people who really need them."

Religious teachings about the environment

Many religions teach that earth, and all life on it, was made by a creator. We should treat it as special, because it doesn't belong to us. Some faiths teach that we have been given a special responsibility to look after it. Some religions have creation stories to explain how the universe and life on earth began. Many believe these stories are completely true. Others think that they are just ways of explaining what humans couldn't hope to understand – even if it was explained to them. Some don't think that the universe was ever created – it's just always existed in some form. Here are some teachings about nature from world faiths.

Christianity – mankind's special place

God created the heavens and the Earth. He separated the sky from the sea and the land. He made plants and trees, beautiful flowers and sweet fruits. He created the stars and the moon – splitting night from day, year from year. He made the birds and sea creatures. Then he made animal life. Each time he made something new he was very pleased with his work. He told all life to make more of their kind.

Then he made a man, and from him a woman. He made them to be like himself. He told them that they should have power over all life. Then he rested. But the man and woman wanted to be in charge of themselves, not just do what God told them. So they disobeyed God. He was angry, he was upset. He made their easy life hard. Unless they came back to him, all life on earth would suffer.

Islam – judgement for all

Allah made the earth a paradise. He made a garden for mankind to live in. Adam was to be his deputy (khalifa), and care for Allah's creation. Adam and Eve lived in the garden. Allah made just one rule: they were to stay away from the tree of knowledge. But they didn't and Allah punished them. They were sent from the garden and then had to work hard to survive. Pain and suffering followed them for their disobedience. Allah sent messengers to turn mankind back to him.

Everything Allah made has a purpose. He keeps all life going. All life follows Allah's law. At the end of life, all are judged by Allah for their actions. Allah gives us freedom, but expects us to choose wisely. The world is Allah's gift to us.

Judaism – everything comes from G-d

The Torah speaks of G-d creating all things. Light in the sky, waters over the earth, and dry land. The sun and moon were put in their place. Then the seas and skies filled with life. All kinds of animals roamed the land. G-d took the dust of the earth, formed man and breathed life into him. He made him master of all living things. From his rib he made woman. G-d saw that what he'd made was good, and so he rested, commanding all life to rest on the seventh day. Adam & Eve were to act for G-d in this world, but chose to act for themselves. They blamed the serpent for turning them away from G-d, but he punished them, and the serpent too.

Hinduism – endless cycles

In Brahma's days, the universe takes a form, in his nights, it becomes nothing. Brahma makes, Vishnu preserves and Shiva destroys. All work together as part of the one God. An endless cycle of birth, death and rebirths takes place – of living things, worlds, the universe itself. One story says that Lord Vishnu, asleep in nothingness was wakened by the sound of the Om. He commands Brahma to make all life. Others say that everything comes from the body of Brahma who, lonely, creates life from himself. When did this begin? A question like this can't be answered. When will it end? No one knows, but when Lord Brahma sleeps, everything will return to nothing. All life is part of the one supreme God, depending on him for its existence. It looks permanent, but that's an illusion. One day everything will no longer be.

Buddhism – everything changes

Some travellers rested under a banyan tree, then cut it down. The Buddha gave them a row. 'Having given you shade like a friend, you then destroyed the friend'. Buddha refused to answer questions like 'how did the world begin' – preferring to try to make it better now. Everything we see is Maya, illusion. Nothing is permanent, including life, the universe and everything in it. Life is going through an endless cycle of birth and rebirth. Eventually it will all pass away. But life's a struggle. Everything's trying to escape this round of rebirths and achieve Nirvana (paradise). It does no one any good to interfere with another living things' struggle, through many lives, towards perfection.

Sikhism – God is all and all is God

Before there was anything there was God. He could not create another God so made the universe instead. He made the creative energy of the universe. Sikhs say in the Mool Mantra, 'Ik ong kar'. One meaning of this is 'The One, who through creative energy, created all that there is'. God made everything and is part of everything. This means that everything is special because it is filled with the spirit of the one God.

PAUSE & RECORD

- Find three similarities between two of the faiths mentioned here. This can either be in their story of how life/the universe began, or how they think we should treat nature.

Although religious people have lots in common, they sometimes disagree about the right thing to do or the best way to do the right thing. There aren't many people (fortunately) who want to harm the environment on purpose, but harm can be caused without it being planned! Sometimes, it's just one choice instead of another which leads to environmental problems.

Muslims

Allah will judge our actions. If we destroy his creation then our judgement will be harsh. Everything in nature has a reason for living. It isn't up to us to decide what lives and dies. We must live in harmony with Allah's creation.

You can care too much about nature. Only Allah should be worshipped. If all you care about is the environment, then you are worshipping nature. You have made it your idol. Humans haven't the power to change nature for better or worse anyway – only Allah can do this. Concentrate on your religious life, not saving dolphins.

Christians

God gave me responsibility for his creation. I'm his steward. It's up to me to make sure I do everything I can to help the environment and do nothing to harm it. Human greed causes trouble – we need to think about other living things too.

God made me in charge of nature – so we should use it for people's benefit. People come first. We can't let environmental worries get in the way of human need. Besides, Christians should try to get people's relationship right with God – that's the first – and only – way to make life better for every living thing. Then we won't have environmental problems.

Jews

G-d made man to have dominion over the earth. This means nurture it and care for it. G-d made us like himself, with the knowledge of good and evil and the power to choose. Nature is in our hands. If we spoil it, we've thrown G-d's gift back in his face.

Yes, G-d's given us dominion, but this means using nature for our own good. Humans are masters of the environment. It's there to make our lives easier. How can you say that the life of a salmon is more important than the comfort, work, power and prosperity that a dam would bring to many people?

Differences of opinion

Hindus

All life is part of God, so how can I mistreat it? All living things come from God and will return to him. It is not my place, a mere speck in the universe, to take control of nature. Shiva chooses when to destroy, not me. I too am part of nature. I should treat it with care, or I too, may come to harm.

Nature's endless cycles are too big to understand. How can I think that my actions will have much effect? We humans must try to live good lives, not worry about saving rain forests. Vishnu preserves all living things. It is big-headed to think that we can interfere with this. We use nature for ourselves – God will see that we don't cause problems.

Sikhs

God is part of all living things. Each time I cut down a tree I show a lack of respect for God's creation. As humans we should behave responsibly towards nature, just like we should behave responsibly towards each other. Also, harming nature might cause harm to people.

But too much concern for the environment might lead to ignoring human needs. Our first responsibility is to each other, to help each other grow in faith. Sometimes what's good for nature and good for humans isn't the same. Humans come first.

Buddhists

All nature struggles towards Nirvana. All life forms are part of the cycle of birth and rebirth. Humans are no different. It is not for us to abuse nature, it has its own rights. We should practise loving kindness to all things, respecting them and valuing them. This is one way to enlightenment.

But everything is an illusion anyway. We should follow a middle path. Not caring too much for nature, nor caring too little. Being too attached to nature gets in the way of spiritual progress. The environment can look after itself.

PAUSE & RECORD

- Choose one of these statements that you agree with. In your own words, explain why.
- From these statements find two examples of an opinion and write them down.

What do you know?

❶ What might be good and bad about the building of a dam?

❷ State one possible *cause* and one *effect* of global warming.

❸ What does the phrase 'environmentally friendly' mean?

❹ Why is recycling a good thing?

❺ Choose one religion. Write one thing it teaches about the environment.

❻ Go back to pages 64 and 65. Draw up a table of things that each of the six religions have in common in their teachings about the environment.

❼ State one belief about the environment which Jews and Christians might have in common.

❽ What do the following words/phrases mean: greenhouse gases; endangered; renewable; recycling; fact; opinion; stewardship; interdependence; dominion; creation.

What do you think?

❶ You live on the banks of a beautiful river. You hear that a dam is to be built which might affect the river. Write a short letter to your MP explaining your views on this. (You can support it or oppose it.)

❷ Produce a short information leaflet on an environmental issue of your choice. Include:

• a title page

• a page explaining what your issue is

• a page of different viewpoints about it

• artwork/newspaper cuttings etc

• your own personal conclusion on the issue.

Display your leaflet in class.

❸ Look through one newspaper for one week. Cut out all the articles about the environment in it. Choose three of these and write your own views about the issue. Display in class.

❹ Choose one of the issues from task 3. In your own words, explain what a follower of each of the religions on pages 64 and 65 might think.

❺ Answer the following question in your own words, giving as many reasons as you can:

Does it matter how humans treat the environment?

Final thoughts

This unit has looked at what we're doing to the environment, why should we care about it and what might happen if we don't.

Answer the following:

In this unit:

a   What have you enjoyed best?

b   What did you not enjoy?

c   How good was your work?

d   What would you have liked to improve?

Now list three questions about environmental issues that you would like to find the answers to.

action INTO

Choose two of the following activities.

❶ You are the Prime Minister. Draw up a plan to persuade people to use public transport or cycle more often.

❷ Draw a diagram of connections showing how you depend on others – including the environment – for your needs.

❸ Access a website which deals with environmental issues. Write a short review of it stating what it's about and what's good and bad about the website.

❹ Write a letter to a follower of one of the religions on pages 64 and 65. Say why they should be concerned about the environment, and why they should help the environment because of the teachings of their religion.

❺ In groups, make a list of one thing you could each do every week to improve the local or global environment. Make these 52 statements into a plan of action for the coming year.

Index